NOVEMBER REIGN

CHAPLAIN CAP

Frank
"Where there is love
there is hope"
CAP

ISBN: 978-1-61244-963-0
LCCN: 2021901145

Halo Publishing International, LLC
8000 W Interstate 10, Suite 600
San Antonio, Texas 78230
www.halopublishing.com

Printed and bound in the United States of America

To those who inspired me to write this book yet will never read it, to those who will read it and totally understand, and to those who will read it and find their own "red" letters that will lead them home.

"LOVE NEVER FAILS."

In loving memory Roseanne Caldwell Woodall
"RAW"

12/7/57 - 4/8/13

Contents

Chapter 1

City Lights

The wind and the vibration and roar of the twin engines on the steel horse hitting the eighty-miles-per-hour mark. There was absolutely nothing in the world that could possibly compare. All Chris could see was the pavement right in front of him, the darkness of night hiding the trees on either side of the road. Up ahead, he saw an opening on both sides as a bridge drew closer. To the left, the moon's reflection danced on the watters. For a moment, he was fixated. He paused to soak in every ounce of beauty that revealed itself in that short moment. Lately, anything beautiful had been few and far between. In the distance, he could see the city lights. Behind the lights, darkness followed.

His course led him back to his hometown. Although, home was much more than a place where he laid his head to rest. This journey, without his knowledge, would take him to a home he never knew existed. But the journey was inevitable.

The lonely road slowly transformed into a busy metropolitan. He needed to stop for gas and maybe a hot cup of coffee. The lights of the gas station lit up like Vegas casino signs, yet not a soul was in sight. He pulled in and kicked down. What a long trip he had already endured. His legs were tight from the stiff sitting position. His arms were numb from the constant vibrations of the road and the 1800 cc steel horse beneath him.

As he dismounted and removed his helmet, all he could think about was the ghost that seemed to be chasing him tonight.

"Not now!" he said to himself as he made his way toward the glass doors that were covered in Marlboro and Coors Light advertisements.

The lights inside seemed to be even brighter than those out-side. As he made his way in, to the right he saw rows of items that ranged from candy to automotive products. To his left were the beer and refreshment coolers. Straight ahead was the cashier counter, and just to the right of that were the coffee and fountain drink machines. He had spent a couple of days on the road. A cup of black coffee would tide him over until he arrived at his destination.

Not a single word was spoken between him and the clerk as his helmet and coffee were set on the counter. He looked up and saw the sign that said Restrooms. He smiled and picked up his things, heading in that direction before paying his gas and coffee bill. Christopher Caldwell was a man of very few words, and those words, over the years, had become fewer and fewer.

In the bathroom, he glanced in the mirror after washing his hands and face. He took a deep breath and gave his reflection a long look. His black and white beard matched the faded colors of his road-worn leather vest, or as bikers referred to it, his "cut." Both were dirty and ragged from the elements he faced in his hard life on the road. This night was no different from the nights previous. He was a man looking at himself in a mirror, searching for the unknown. What lay ahead of him was still unclear. All that he was sure of was where the lost highway had taken him over the years since he left home. He dried his hands and took one last look at the dirt and grime in the reflection. He took a sip of his coffee and opened the door to exit the restrooms.

Still in his own world of thought, he exited to find himself in a brand-new environment. Same clerk, same lights, and same music. He looked up and over toward the clerk and found the young female cashier. She was standing with her arms raised, tears streaming down her cheeks. Two masked gunmen were screaming for her to empty the cash registers. One began counting down seconds as he looked at his watch. The other stood behind the counter with her. While calling out the remaining time, the first masked intruder crept down the side aisle, watching the entrances. Both were armed.

A moment of panic struck both intruders once Chris was in sight, and they both began yelling at him to get on the floor. The gunman watching the door began moving closer to him, his weapon pointed at Chris's head. Both men wore red bandanas to hide their identities. They shared a similar profile: medium build, Caucasian. The doorman was slightly more muscular, and he raced closer to Chris, becoming more and more animated and aggressive with his actions. His anger was like a pot of boiling water, spewing over the surface of a stove, spilling on the kitchen floor.

"I said to get on the damn ground! Now!" he screamed.

Chris looked at him and then glanced at the other behind the counter. The gunman behind the counter was busy pulling cash from the registers rapidly, trying to hold the book bag in the other hand. The other one was still yelling as he closed in on Chris. The weapon was a Glock 17. A good weapon. Mostly plastic. A standard 9mm. Very accurate, durable. Holding a seventeen-round clip, hence the name. The man's gun hand was trembling, his index finger pressed to the trigger. He was moments away from firing the first round. His first mistake was carelessly moving too fast toward Chris, who still had coffee in his right hand and his helmet in his left.

He turned to put his coffee on the counter and said with a smile, "Look, Brother, there are a few ways that this can end…"

The gunman's anger visibly rose.

"Shut your hole, old man! I said, get on your damn knees. I won't say it a third time!"

The weapon was now directly in front of Chris's face, less than a foot away. The gunman's arm was fully extended. Second mistake. With one fast engagement, Chris moved to his left. His right hand grabbed the barrel of the Glock. His left hand swung the helmet toward the man's extended arm, striking him at the elbow. After one fluid motion, the weapon was now in Chris's possession. He cleared the chamber and calculated his next move: fire the weapon at the man who now lay screaming on the floor beneath him due to the painful broken limb, or turn his attention toward the man behind the counter. He chose the latter.

"Now, you and I have two choices, my friend," he said while slowly drawing nearer to the counter.

The man behind the counter was in a panic, stumbling backward, knocking down rows of lottery tickets and cigarette packs as he frantically attempted to figure out how to clutch the money bag and raise his own weapon to defend himself against the mysterious hero heading toward him.

Chris said in a calm and steady voice, "Choice number one: Raise that weapon and die. Or choice number two: Lay it on the counter and put your nose to the ground."

While giving these instructions carefully, he could not keep his face from forming an abnormally cheerful smile.

The Glock in his hand was fixed in a protective firing position. Like a picture from a manual covering the topic of close-quarter combat, he held the weapon at chest level, his elbows tucked in toward his body. His index finger was to the side of the trigger housing, relaxed but ready to fire if need arose. His eyes locked in on his prey. His movements were decisive and calculated.

The gunman looked in the direction of his companion, who was still on the floor in pain, and then back at Chris. He laid the weapon on the counter and hit the floor.

"You have to call the police, sweetheart," Chris said calmly and directly as he directed his attention to the terrified clerk. "It's okay, sweets. Nobody is gonna hurt you. But I need your help now. Can you do that for me, please? I need you to call nine-one-one and get us some assistance. Can you do that for me?"

She moved forward to the front of the counter and hit a little red panic button under it. Then she moved back into her place, her hands still in the air.

"Well, that works, too. You can put your hands down, though. I'm not gonna hurt you," he said with a laugh.

After that, she dropped to her knees, her face in her hands now as she sobbed uncontrollably.

Chris leaned back on the counter and picked up his coffee, swallowing a large gulp. He reached into his cut and pulled out a cigar case, pulling one from its place and biting the end off. He never took his eyes off the two criminals who now lay on the floor. He lit his cigar and waited for company to arrive.

It's about to get interesting, he thought to himself.

He laid the weapon on the counter and pulled out his wallet, removing a ten-dollar bill from the worn leather—two dollars for the coffee and eight for the gas he planned to get for his bike. Looking up, he watched as several squad cars began filing into position to secure the area outside. He took a nice draw from his cigar and watched as the officers began to swarm like angry hornets in the parking lot. He stayed mounted in place behind the counter, leaving his hands in full view of all the cameras inside the store as well as the entrance doors to the front and both sides.

The officers made their entrance, weapons ready to fire. At this moment, all of their weapons were aimed at the bearded man wearing black jeans and leathers, who was leaning on the counter and drawing yet another smoke from his Gurkha cigar.

"Get your hands on your head!" the lead officer commanded.

Chris slowly took a knee, his cigar in his lips and his hands behind his head, and said to the officers who were moving in to scan the scene, "There are two of them, one behind the counter with me and one to the left of you on the floor. There's a very upset young lady back here, as well."

The lead officer secured the three men with his drawn weapon as the assisting officers began applying cuffs to the two gunmen. The man lying in front of the counter began screaming from the pain of his fractured right arm. One officer took the young cashier to safety, and another began to cuff Chris, who offered no resistance. His money was still on the counter. His Indian was still parked and thirsty for petrol at pump number eight. His coffee, which was now room temperature, was on the counter beside the Glock 17. The officers led him and the other two men out and into the squad cars. The night had only begun.

Chapter 2

Old Friends

The smells of body odor, cigarette smoke, and stale coffee lingered in the air. A half-eaten McDonald's cheeseburger was moldy and forgotten under the passenger's seat. Each crucial ingredient combined to form the interesting aroma of the squad car. There was not much room for Chris's legs between the protective roll cage and the rear seat. To make things worse, the officer hadn't felt the need to uncuff him before forcing him into the squad car.

The overweight officer struggled to sit down in the driver's seat and barked at Chris, "What's your name?"

Chris offered nothing but silence.

"Did you hear me, boy? Or do you have too much grease in your ears?"

Chris remained silent.

The officer turned his absurdly obese body as best as he could, giving Chris his most intimidating glare.

"Are you deaf or just stupid?" he snapped while attempting to adjust his seat yet again.

The officer held his glare on his captive through the bulletproof screen. Nothing could break his gaze.

Suddenly, a female officer's voice, which came from just outside the car, interrupted the awkward tension between the two.

"Officer Nelson, that will be enough. Let's get this man out of those cuffs. The clerk says he was responsible for restraining the two in custody."

Officer Nelson looked back at her and then back at the man in his mirror, his face turning red and the veins in his neck growing larger.

"Yeah, okay, Sergeant, but I still don't have his name. I need it to run on the NCIC," he said, smirking.

"It's okay. I know his name. Christopher Caldwell, age forty-two, born August second, nineteen seventy-four," she snapped back.

Both men turned to look at the female sergeant who was standing roughly four feet from the car.

Chris received help getting out of the squad car, and Officer Nelson removed the cuffs, being unnecessarily rough while jerking them off. Chris only nodded a thank-you and did not show any sign of discomfort.

"Hey, Sandy," Chris said with a smile.

"Hey, Chris. How are you? You passing through or staying a while this time?" she said while stepping forward to shake his hand out of professionalism.

"Not really sure. I have to go to the FARM and see about some things."

"I heard about your mama. I'm sorry, Chris. She was a real sweet lady. I miss seeing her in town. She was always smiling."

"Thank you, Sandy. I miss her, too. It's just not the same down here anymore," he said as he looked down the highway and off into the distance.

"Well, I need to get some basic information from you in case we need to follow up on tonight's excitement. Not bad, by the way. Those boys didn't know what they were dealing with."

"Just lost kids searching, Sandy. It's sad. But what can you do? Right?"

"You could have killed those boys, and nobody would have thought negatively of you Chris," she added.

"I would have," he responded, then removed a card from his wallet and handed it to her. "Can I go? I need to get to the FARM. It has been a long ride."

"Yeah, you're good to go. Stay in touch, Chris. Robby would love to see you. Oh, and tell the Boys that I said hello," she said with a loving smile.

He took her hand again in both of his and said, "Good to go, then. Tell Ro that I'll catch him before I leave town."

With that, he turned back to his motorcycle, which had been patiently waiting for him during the chaos. The cash from earlier was stuck under his helmet, along with a note: Thanks for the help tonight, Preach. Fill her up, on me. It was signed S.D. He looked back toward the squad cars. Sergeant Sandra Dickerson, aka Sandy, was leaning on her car and looked up with a shy grin. He put the cash in his pocket and filled up his tank. Once his helmet was secure, he cranked the steel horse and disappeared into the night.

As he departed from the city, light pollution faded and the road darkened, revealing what seemed to be a billion stars in the night sky. As he drew closer to a large, green, metal bridge at the county line, out of the corner of his eye, he noticed a flash of bright red, white, and blue lights lighting up his rear-view mirrors. This was followed by the sound of a siren speeding toward him. He glanced into his rear-view mirrors, then looked back at the road once more. He was less than fifty yards away from the next county, but he slowed to a stop and pulled to the side of the road.

"Put your hands on your head!" a voice yelled over the loud-speaker of a patrol car.

Chris slowly placed his hands on his head. He could hear the car doors open and the sound of two officers moving into position. The assisting officer was to his right, the lead officer to his left. Their outlines blocked the lights in his mirrors. As they approached him, it became easier to see facial features.

"Step off of your bike and keep your hands on your head," the lead officer commanded as he moved into position to do a safety pat down.

"You must like rubbing men's legs," Chris joked.

He slowly turned to face the officers. The other officer was standing several feet away to the left, his hand on his weapon, prepared to draw it if needed.

"Nah, just sissy boys like you," the officer patting him down replied.

Chris slowly took his hands from his head and reached slowly into his cut, keeping his eyes trained on the assisting officer.

"Mind if I smoke? It's been an interesting night," he said as he fired up his Zippo torch, not caring about their answer.

The officer was still standing only a few arm's lengths away. Their eyes were now locked in on one another. It was as if they were intently playing the staring game. The second officer was standing readily. As they stood there, another squad car pulled up beside them slowly and parked just to the front side of Chris's bike, blocking any possible exit. Chris could hear the driver's side door open and footsteps coming in from his rear side.

"You boys gonna stand there all night? Kiss or shoot? I've seen y'all dance before. Might as well shoot," the husky voice playfully said, breaking the silence.

Just as he drew closer, the officer standing in front of Chris reached out to lock arms in a tight, friendly grasp. Laughing together, the officer pulled Chris into a tight bear hug.

"How's it been, Ro?" Chris said as he took a draw from his cigar. "It's been a long while, Brother."

Chris blew the smoke out. He turned to his right to offer a similar handshake. The man standing beside him towered over his six-feet-two frame.

Ro reached down and picked up Chris.

"How the heck are you, lil Brother?" he said as he put him back down. He straightened Chris's cut and offered a big smile. "Got ya some more patches on your leather, eh?"

"Yeah. Ol' dogs don't change," Chris replied.

"Well, old is the truth." The man laughed.

"Will, how's Jenny?" Chris asked, half smiling back.

"Oh, you know Jenny. Same gal, same city, same problems, but overall we are good. The boys are good. How long are you in town?" Will responded.

"Not sure, to be honest. I need to get to the FARM."

"I hear ya, Brother. Sandy told us that you were headed that way. I wanted to catch you first."

Chris was now looking at Will, knowing that the conversation was much deeper than just two old pals chatting.

"Why, Will? What's up?" he asked, feeling chills run up his spine.

"Things do change, Brother. Just go in there knowing that," Will said, looking down the road and back at Chris.

The three men stood there silently for a second, and the third officer cleared his throat to remind them that he was still present.

"Oh, stand down, Jimmy. This is an old friend. To us and to this town. Let me introduce you to Christopher 'Preach' Caldwell." Will said this as he placed his hand on Chris's shoulder.

Chris looked at Will's hand and back up at him.

The younger officer reached out to shake Chris's hand and said, "Oh wow! You knew my brother. I can remember you from when I was a little kid."

Chris looked at Jimmy's name plate and asked, "James King? You're Matty's little brother? How is that old rattlesnake?"

Jimmy looked at the other officers as if to get permission to respond, then said, "Dead. They found his body in the river last winter. No one knows what happened."

He looked down as he finished his statement.

Chris bowed his head and then spoke. "I'm sorry, kid. Matty was a true friend."

The four men shook hands again and said their goodbyes. Chris hit the ignition switch on his bike, hearing it thunder underneath him. He watched the two squad cars pull out and head back into town. Once their driving lights were well off in the distance, he secured his helmet and headed toward the FARM.

Chapter 3

Fourth Watch

The sign said Dobson Gap. It was a four-way stop. The direction Chris was headed would take him through a scenic mountain view. To the right, the route would take him away from the past. Forward would lead him into the Cloudlands, which would cross over into Alabama. To the left was the FARM. Turning left might lead him to some answers to all of the puzzling questions in his mind.

He stopped at the stop sign, steadied his bike, and looked north, to his right. The darkness enveloped the curvy road. Behind him, the interstate and bright city lights glimmered. The rising sun was slowly beginning to outshine the artificial lights of the city. He was running behind schedule. Although he had no pressing agenda, he had hoped to arrive at the FARM by now. He had also been hoping to maybe catch up on some sleep before the new day began. He looked at his watch, which now read 04:45. Sunrise would be in just over an hour.

"Fourth watch," he said to himself.

Turning to the left, he twisted the throttle, hearing the roar of his bike as it picked up speed. A few short miles more, and he would be at his destination.

The FARM was not an agricultural plot of land. While there were rows of crops—corn, okra, tomatoes, cucumbers, bell peppers, peanuts, beans of various types, and maybe potatoes—along with rows of apple trees, strawberries, and blueberry patches, the FARM was so much more. On the outside looking in, it appeared to be a custom automobile and motorcycle shop, specializing in rat rods and custom motorcycles. It was fronted by a fifties-style barbershop, a tattoo studio, and a legendary Irish pub called The Belle.

Towering high above the pub itself was an operating steeple bell that rang every hour. It had once belonged to an old Pentecostal church before it was burned down by some kids smoking in the lower rooms during one of C. L. Woods's now-famous revivals.

Behind the sixteen-feet-high fence line was the secret of Dobson County: one hundred and twenty acres of tree line. Horse stables, two man-made lakes, an old Confederate cemetery, and three ten-thousand-square-feet metal buildings filled with cars, bikes, and a divine gym. Another building sat in the center of it all, a flagpole at its entrance. Come sunrise, it would support the red, white, and blue. A yellow flag that said Don't tread on me was flying proudly. As if that were not enough, a white-and-black trimmed flag that showed a raven holding a rose in its beak, sitting royally upon a skull with crossbones, beat wildly in the wind, the words LOST BOYS MC within its ranks.

The sign of The Belle was still flashing with a multitude of neon alcohol signs. The billboard was still on, but at this hour in the morning, only a skeleton crew of employees would be cleaning up from the night prior. Chris knew that regardless of this, the front door would be unlocked and open.

As he backed his bike into a space, he took a deep breath an debated his next move. It had been a few years since he had last stepped through those doors. He unstrapped his helmet and secured it to the forward controls of his chrome and ashen white horse.

The place looked exactly the same as it did so many years ago as he made his entrance. A young man, probably in his late teens, stood at the front sweeping up.

"We're closed, man," the kid said without looking up.

Chris stopped to look at the pictures on the front wall and said, "It's okay, kid. I know the owner."

The wall held rows of old photographs. Some of them were decades old. Smiling faces, bikes, women, and friendships, or rather, a Brotherhood that would never fade away like the paper the pictures were printed on.

The kid looked up at the man standing in his way and started to say something, but then he saw the patches on the back of his cut. They proudly presented Lost Boys on the top rocker and had the same raven, skull, and crossbones that flew on the flag at the far end of the bar and appeared in almost every photo on the wall.

Chris found a picture with four men standing tall together in their leathers. They were connected like a chain, their arms around each other's necks. They were all smiling. Brothers that even blood could not create. In the center was a younger version of Chris. He put his hand on the picture, wiping some dust from it, then turned to walk past the kid, who was still watching the man invading his workspace.

He went through the double doors that led into the main room, which had a large horseshoe-shaped bar and a long bar that ran down the right of it, going from one side of the building to the other. Stools sat up on high-top tables. There was a pretty young woman on the far left, near the bandstand. She looked up and saw him, then turned and hurried herself back into the billiards room, vanishing out of sight. An extremely large ponytailed man with a beard was cleaning up the bottles that spread across the wall. The jukebox was still playing an old 38 Special song.

Chris pulled up a stool and leaned his elbows on the bar top. The smells of spilled beer, fruit, smoke, and hot steam rose from the glass washer behind the bar.

The man behind the bar looked in the mirror and glimpsed Chris.

"Sorry, Brother, but we closed two hours ago," he said faintly.

"It's okay. I'm not here to drink. Is Cleo still around?" Chris politely asked.

The bartender came over to where Chris was leaning against the bar. He took a long look at him. He had a rocks glass and a clean towel in his hand. After looking at Chris's leather—the patches that proudly read Man of Valor and Original Eight, the name patch that read Preach—he opened a locked cabinet, removing a bottle of Platinum Jameson Irish Whiskey, and poured two tall shots side by side.

"This one's for Cleo," he said, knowing that Chris was speaking in club code.

"How's it going, Wayne?" Chris said as he tapped his glass on the bar top and then against the other man's glass.

"Hey, Preach. Where you been, Bro?" Wayne responded.

"Long ride..." Chris said as he slammed the whiskey in one swallow.

"You need a cot?"

"Yeah, if one's open."

The big man laughed and said, "If there's not one, I'll open one up for you, lil Brother."

The two men grasped arms tightly, and Wayne motioned for Chris to follow him. They went through the kitchen doors and out the back door, then made their way across the small court-yard, heading toward the middle building with the flagpole in front. Two men were making themselves busy, positioning the flags to raise as the sun peeked through the horizon. A third man was standing at ready, waiting to blow his bugle to announce the morning sunrise. Once inside the building, Chris saw two men playing a game of pool, but neither of them looked up to take notice of Wayne and Chris. A petite red-headed girl was sleeping on a couch to the right side of the front room. Three large-screen TVs were playing sports talk shows that covered the day's highlights.

The two men continued through another set of doors and down a long hallway. There were doors to rooms on both sides. Wayne opened one of the doors to the left, and the sound of snoring boomed from within.

"That's Bear. I wouldn't do that to my worst enemy!" he joked.

A few more doors down, he opened a door on the right side of the hall. Chris could see in, and six feet could be seen from underneath the covers.

Wayne closed the door with a smile and said, "Oops…"

The next door opened to a vacant room.

"Here ya go. I'll leave you to it. There's a shower and a toilet down the hall. You want me to send you anything?" Wayne said before turning back down the hall to leave.

Chris knew that Wayne was referring to drugs, booze, girls, or all of the above, so he said, "Nah, I'm good. A shower and some sleep."

"All right then, lil Brother. I'll see you later on," he said, then shut the door and headed back down the hallway, whistling an old Irish folk song, tapping each door along the way to irritate the occupants.

Chris walked over to the bed and sat down. Looking around the room, he saw a small dresser, a round mirror on the wall above it, and a small closet. Not much to look at, but it was better than the hard ground outside. Standing up, he walked over to the mirror and looked.

"Dang, son, you look like a lost dog."

A knock came at the door, and he walked over to see who it was. The cute girl from the bar was standing there holding a fresh towel and a bottle of Irish whiskey.

"Wayne told me to bring this to you," she said, looking up at Chris. "You need anything else?"

"What's your name, sweets?" Chris asked as he looked at her.

"Marla."

"Well, it's nice to meet you, Ms. Marla. Thanks for the supplies."

He took the items from her hands and politely excused himself, shutting the door behind him.

***

She stared at the door for a moment and then turned to go back down the hallway. She stopped about midway to look back, and she thought about going back to knock again. Changing her mind, she headed for the exit doors of the clubhouse, heading back to The Belle and leaving Chris behind.

"What are you doing back so quickly?" Wayne asked her as she stepped back into the bar area.

"He took his things and shut the door," she answered.

"Are you serious? Hmm…" Wayne was puzzled. He looked back at Marla. "Well, okay then. Let's roll."

The two walked out the front doors and locked up. Marla climbed onto the back of Wayne's motorcycle. He started his Harley Shovelhead, and the two rode off to the west side of town.

***

Chris took off his leather cut and folded it. Then he removed his t-shirt and placed his palms on the dresser, his triceps and back muscles flexed as he stared once again at his reflection. His hair was pulled tightly into a samurai bun. His beard was longer than normal and was dirty from the road. His arms were tattooed, and his back was covered in a multitude of scars. His face was scarred from battle, as well. He opened the bottle of whiskey and took a long drink.

"I have to get a shower before I crash," he said to himself as he opened the door and made his way down the hall, towel, whiskey, and leather saddlebag in hand.

He opened the door to the small bathroom. It had the bare essentials. It was a simple setup with a shower-tub combo, a toilet, and a sink with a mirror. He reached in to turn on the water. After stepping into the water, which was hot yet extremely refreshing, he took his time cleaning the road off his body. He randomly took long gulps of whiskey. He could already feel the alcohol's effects on his body. It had been a few days on the road. He would shower and then get some rest. He reached into his saddlebag and retrieved a prescription bottle of pain pills. He shook a few into his palm and popped them in his mouth, chasing them down with Jameson. He knew that they would call Church later that day, but right now more whiskey and some much-needed rest.

Chapter 4

The FARM

"What do you think made him come back, Sammy?" a tall, lean sentry guard asked.

"Your guess is as good as mine, Bro. But this is gonna rile up the Brothers. The last time he was home was at his mama's funeral. He just sort of vanished after that," responded an older man standing along the perimeter fence.

"I always heard stories about him, but I wasn't patched when he left," the tall sentry guard said.

"All that I know, Stick, is that he used to be pretty high up on the food chain. But when we blinked, he was like a ghost. Gone," Sammy said.

At that very moment, the sound of high-powered rifle fire came from the far side of the compound, echoing through the early morning sky.

"Someone scheduled to shoot on the range this early?" Stick questioned.

"Not sure. Better go see."

The two men raced toward the far rear building.

***

"Hit!" the shot spotter exclaimed.

Chris took a deep breath, exhaled, and fired the .308 again.

"Hit!"

"The scope is dialed in right, to the northeast," Chris noted.

The shot spotter wrote down the remark on his pad as Chris fired off three more rounds.

"One thousand meters, all center mass. Nice," the spotter remarked as he noted the range on his pad.

The two sentry guards came walking in from behind.

Chris acknowledged them with a nod and said, looking up from his scope again, "Two more rounds, and we will clear the range, boys."

The men put on safety ears and stood back. Far off in the distance, a green flag signaled to continue fire.

"Thirteen hundred meters, Preach," the spotter informed Chris.

Chris adjusted the scope and took a moment to scan down the line of fire before returning his eye to the scope. His finger rested steadily on the trigger. Once again, he took a deep breath, then exhaled as he squeezed and fired.

"Hit!"

A final round fired off.

"Hit!"

Chris checked the weapon and cleared the chamber before handing the spotter the rifle.

"Thanks again for the assist," the spotter said as he reached out to shake Chris's hand.

"No worries, Bro. It's been a minute," Chris said, smiling as he spoke to the range spotter.

He turned toward the two men behind him and reached out to take the older of the two's hand. Then, keeping his eyes on Sammy, he reached out to shake the other man's hand and said, "Hey, Sammy. How's the leg?"

"Oh man, it's as good as ever." He laughed as he pulled up his right pant leg to display a high-tech prosthetic. Then, done with the small talk, he asked, "What has you back?"

"I'll explain at Church. Anyone at the shop I might know?" Chris asked curiously.

Sammy looked down as he thought about it.

"Beau, Dutch, and Cowboy in the garage, and most likely Rocky in the office. Anyone know you were coming?"

Chris just grabbed his saddlebag and started toward the shop.

"Nope."

The three men began walking together. Stick and Sammy both looked at one another and then back at Chris, who was taking the lead. The sound of torque wrenches and the sparking buzz of a wielder in the rear of the building could be heard. Beau and Dutch were overlooking some last-minute changes on a custom project they were working on. Cowboy was busy welding a frame. Beau and Dutch looked up as they heard the men enter but did not seem to be concerned. Sammy and Chris headed past them and went toward the doors to the office, but Stick made his way to the two looking over a design on the computer screen.

***

"Dude! Do you guys know who that was?" Stick asked in childlike excitement.

They both looked back at the men leaving the room.

"Should we?" Dutch snapped.

"Well, umm…that's Preach walking up ahead of Sammy," Stick snapped back at his friend.

They all turned around again to watch the doors close behind Sammy.

"I thought he was dead," Beau said.

"Nah, but I didn't think we would see him again," Dutch added as he took out his phone and walked away to make a call.

***

"Well, aren't you a sight for sore eyes?" said a voice from behind Chris and Sammy as they made their way into the office area.

"I suppose to some," Chris joked, turning to walk toward the pretty young lady sitting at a desk. "You look good, Rocky. It's been a long time, girl."

He reached down to hug her in her chair.

"Oh, Chris, I've missed you. Sandy texted me last night and told me that you were home. I woke up Jaybo, and he was rather surprised. What's going on?" she said as she looked up at the

32

ghost standing in front of her. "Not that it really matters. Just glad to see you."

"I have some business in town, and then I'll get back on the road. Have they called Church yet?" he asked as he looked around the office.

"Yeah, Church tonight at eighteen hundred hours. The Sisters are making plans now."

"All right then. I'll see you guys tonight."

***

Sammy and Rocky watched him leave, looking at each other in combined puzzlement.

"What's that about?" Sammy asked out loud, not necessarily looking for an answer.

"I don't know, Sam. But you better call Mo, tell him that he has company en route."

"Yeah, you're probably right," he said, already dialing his cellphone.

***

Once back on the road, Chris's thoughts were jumping from one thought to the next. Memories of the past were dancing around in his mind.

The sign up ahead said Valley Town, AL. He continued down the two-lane road. The smells of a mountain stream and wild kudzu filled his senses. Two miles farther down, he took a left on Williams Road, and after crossing the railroad tracks, he swung another left onto Cemetery Road. He took his time looking at the scenery as he drew closer to the old Baptist church. After taking a right and heading toward the gravestones, he stopped and kicked down.

He looked around at all the little flags. Some were American, red, white, and blue, while some were old red-and-blue Confederate stripes. There were rows of plastic flowers next to hundreds of headstones. Row after row. He walked over to a set of headers. The first of them read John James McGregor and Anne Bell McGregor. The second header read Rose Anne Caldwell. He reached into his jeans pocket and took out a coin, placing it heads-up on the header.

"May the ferryman be quick about his business. Godspeed." Then, holding back tears, he said, "Hey, Mama, sure do miss you down here."

He placed his hand on the cold stone header. His mind raced through a dozen memories of his mother's smile. Her laugh. The wisdom behind the words she had gently spoken to him.

"It's just not the same anymore, Mama. I don't know what I'm doing anymore. I don't know why I came back," he said as he fought back the tears. "But I'm here. What now?"

He looked up into the cloudy sky, then leaned down to kiss the header, bowed his head as if to say a quick prayer, and then walked back to his bike. Though he didn't give any indication that he noticed it, he saw something on the far-off hill to his right. As he looked beyond the old church, he saw the reflection of the sun as it bounced off what he assumed was binoculars or possibly a high-powered rifle scope. He was hoping for binoculars, or maybe even a long-distance camera lens. He put on his helmet and hit the ignition switch, the roar of his horse echoing through the pines. As he rode around the circle loop and got back onto Cemetery Road, he looked up toward the hill line, convinced someone was watching him. But why? That was the question. He turned and headed south, crossing over the old Dam Bridge and riding through the curves that led to the town ahead. Although he knew no one was tailing him, he also knew it would not be long before whoever was up on the hill presented himself.

Chapter 5

Wally's

Valley Town had not changed much over the years. The court-house sat right in the middle of the main road. To its left was the same old jail building that had not been used in decades. To the right were Case's ACE True Value Hardware, Dollar General, Liz's flower shop, and Fuller's barbershop, and tucked away in the far corner was a little diner called Wally's Grill and Malts.

Chris parked his bike facing the main road, as always, and headed to the doors of the diner. Upon entering, he could hear the busy sounds of chatter, laughter, forks scraping plates, dishes being cleared from tables, and waitresses calling out orders to the line cooks in the back. He made his way to the far corner, where he had a full view of the front doors and the large windows looking out into the street. The smells of bacon on the grill and burgers being flipped reached him and his growling stomach.

"Whatcha gonna have?"

"Coffee. Black, please," he said, answering the woman behind the counter.

She grabbed a pot from the warmer and a fresh mug to fill up. She placed it on the counter and busied herself, not noticing the man sitting behind the menu.

"I'll be right back, doll," she said as she raced off to fetch an armload of food from the line window.

He laid down his menu and took a drink of his coffee, which, considering the stale taste of it, had most likely been sitting in that pot for several hours. Truth be told, that was exactly how he preferred his Joe.

He sat quietly for a few minutes, waiting on the waitress to return, and when she did, he said, "Six eggs, no yellows. Hash browns with white gravy, and if you have them, I'd like some freshly sliced tomatoes, please."

She wrote down the order without looking up at him and turned to call out the order, but then she stopped short and turned around, dropping her pen and tablet on the register.

"Christopher Caldwell! Oh my goodness! What in the heavens are you doing, boy?" she screamed as she made her way to him on the other side of the counter.

"Mrs. Dolly. How are you, ma'am?" he said as she grabbed him and hugged him tightly.

"It's going, I suppose. Walter left me for a long-haired hippy last spring," she said.

He was surprised.

"Yeah, he decided to run off to heaven with Jesus," she joked. "It's been hard without him. But he needed a vacation."

"Dolly, I'm sorry. I didn't know," he said, giving her hand a squeeze.

"Oh boy, he sure did love you. He always knew you'd come back sooner or later. He used to watch that window for your bike to pull in." She reached up and popped him on the head. "So, where you been?"

He looked around the diner and then back at her. He reached into his cut, took out the crumbled-up paper, and placed it on the counter, the writing face-up.

"What is this, Chris?" she asked as she looked at the message that had been inked in red.

"I'm really not sure, Dolly. But it's Mama's handwriting, isn't it?" he questioned as he watched her eyes study the paper. "I was over in Murphy when I got this. I was coming out of a bar pretty tore up, and it was taped to my seat. I got angry at first. I tossed it on the pavement, but as I started to pull off, something deep inside me made me pick it back up. Here I am a month later."

Dolly picked up the brown paper. The message Come Home was written on it. She studied it and put it back down, then looked back up at Chris.

"Sweetheart, your mama has been in heaven for three years. You still lived here then. That can't possibly be her handwriting," she said sympathetically.

"I know, Dolly. That's what I've tried to tell myself over and over. I tried to ignore it. But then I found this." He pulled out a letter addressed to him from December 2012. "This was five months before Mama passed. Look at the handwriting. It's hers. Same lines. Same red ink. Same basic message. Come Home."

"Well! Why don't you look at that?" she said as she compared the writing. "What's your next move, Chris?"

"Not really sure. I came to see if Walter could make any sense of it," he said as he looked out the windows of the diner.

"I'm sorry, sweetheart. What can I do to help?" she asked, open concern in her voice.

"I have no clue," he said as he became more distracted by the street beyond the window.

"I'll be right back."

He made his way out the doors and into the street. Just outside, beyond the parked cars, a pretty young woman, probably in her early twenties, was briskly walking away from a young man wearing the colors of a motorcycle club called the Skulls.

***

"Come on, baby. All I want is your number," begged a young man who was dressed in jeans and a leather jacket flying the colors and bones of his MC.

"Well, I'm not wanting to give it to you," the young girl snapped, trying her best to get to her car, her hands full of brown folders, a computer bag on her shoulder.

"I won't bite you, baby. Just let me take you out," he persistently pushed, not allowing her to get into her car.

"And I said no to you three times already. I'm sorry, but I'm not interested," she said with a shy but determined smile, seemingly trying her best to remain polite and calm at the same time.

The young biker put his hand on the door of her car, stopping it from opening.

"I'm getting tired of this game, Anna. I'll make you mine. But I'd rather you choose to be mine. Either way, I will have you," he barked sternly, becoming more enraged.

"Well, Ricky Saunders, that isn't how things work in the real world. You can't make me be anything that I don't wish to be. And with the way you're treating me now, why would you think I'd ever choose to be your friend?"

She reached for the door handle again, not looking up at him, fear in her eyes.

"Let me in my car, Ricky! Now!" she said under her breath, seemingly trying her best to not make a scene.

"You know I'm a Skull, Anna. I can do whatever I want. Who is gonna stop me? Daddy?" he said.

She looked up at him, tears beginning to form in her eyes, but before she could respond, Chris decided it was time to step in.

***

"Hey, Anna. They need you in Wally's."

He stood behind Ricky, looking at Anna.

"And just who exactly are you, Bro?" Ricky snapped.

"Well, first of all, I'm not your Brother. Secondly, the young lady has asked you nicely to back off. Now she is being summoned into Wally's. You can move so that she can do her business, or I can gladly assist you in moving. That's up to you," Chris said as he reached out to take Anna's hand and help her onto the curb.

She walked past Ricky, looking at Chris as she made her way toward the doors of the diner.

Ricky began stepping in Chris's direction.

"You're getting in my way, ol' man. You're wearing the wrong colors in Valley Town. Lost Boys are forgotten. Skullys rule now."

He started to put his hand on Chris's shoulder, but Chris turned his body into Ricky's, making a S with Ricky's wrist, arm,

38

and shoulder. He pressed his pinky slowly toward his chest, and the pain forced Ricky to one knee.

"Not really sure what a Skully is, but this ol' man is about to pull off his belt and send you back to your daddy with a red butt."

Chris let Ricky go and reached down to offer him a hand. Ricky jumped up to his feet, grabbing his hurt hand.

"I'll kill you for that!" he screamed.

"Nobody is getting killed today, son. Go home," Chris said as he turned his back to Ricky.

He opened the doors to the diner without looking back at the boy standing on the curb.

***

"Who in the world is that man, Dolly?" Anna asked as she stared out the windows, watching the two men outside.

"That's Chris Caldwell. Most people 'round here call him 'Preach.' He was friends with your parents a long time ago," Dolly answered as she helped unload the folders from Anna's arms before moving away from her.

***

Chris walked over to Dolly, still looking at Anna.

"She looks just like Emma. I thought it was her until I realized that's not possible," he said to Dolly, and then he walked straight toward the timid girl and said, "Hello, Anna. I'm Christopher. I am close friends with your mama, and your daddy is one of the best friends I ever had." He looked intensely at the young woman. "You are Anna Elizabeth Callaway. I held you the night that you were born."

He reached out to shake her hand.

"Pleased to meet you. My grandpa doesn't talk much about my parents, so I have never heard about you," she said as she looked up at the man standing beside the counter.

"I'm sure he has his reasons," he said with a smile. "Henry is a good man. It looks like he raised you up to be a fine lady. Would you care to have a bite to eat so you can give Junior out there time to saddle up and leave?"

She looked out the window. Ricky was pulling out on his bike.

"He used to be a nice boy. He doesn't mean harm. He just likes to play tough," she said as she sat down in a booth.

Chris joined her. They sat and talked for a while. Then he walked her to her car. He glanced at his watch. It was 16:32.

"I'll see you soon, Ms. Anna. Be sure to tell your grandpa hello for me," he said.

He walked over to his bike, started it up, and looked back at Anna one last time. Then he waved at Dolly. He waved once more at the two ladies as he rode off.

As he headed back out of town, six bikes flying their red colors pulled up alongside him. The leader of the pack pointed toward a curb. Chris nodded and pulled to the side, the other bikers pulling in behind him. He turned and sat sideways on the saddle. Three of the men fell behind him, two of them went to each side of him, and the leader walked in front of Chris. He took off his helmet and the red bandana covering his face.

"Hey, Brother," he said as he reached to shake Chris's hand.

Chris reached into his pocket and took out a cigar and his Zippo. He never once took his eyes off of the man standing in front of him. He lit his cigar and let out a cloud of smoke.

"Seems to be the theme of the afternoon," Chris said with a hint of sarcasm, "but like I said once already today, I'm not your Brother. I'm guessing that your boy ran home crying to Daddy about the mean ol' man in town square."

"Rick said he ran into a Lost Boy causing problems," the man said as he studied Chris. "What are you doing back, Preach?"

The man crossed his arms to look more foreboding.

"Your kid was being rude to a young lady at Wally's, so I sent him home."

Chris looked to his left and right. The men surrounding him all appeared to be in their twenties.

"You open up a daycare, Rockhound?"

The two men looked at each other and both gave a courtesy laugh, neither one really humored. Rockhound motioned for his boys to stand down, his expression changing to one of grave seriousness. Chris could feel the tension rise. Rockhound pulled on his beard, seeming to look for the words to say next.

Chris's eyes caught the odd sight of a large black raven landing on the fence thirty yards away, on the other side of the road.

A Harbinger, he thought to himself, but then he focused back on the words coming out of Rockhound's mouth when he snapped his figures in front of Chris's face to get his attention.

"Hey! Are you paying attention?" he grumbled. "Look, Preach, we go way back, so I'm going to let this slide. But how about you follow Old Federal Highway back out of town and stay wherever it is that you've been the last three years."

He made his way back to his bike, his boys following suit.

"We needed you. And you disappeared. Do it again," he said as he cranked his bike and secured his headgear.

"I'll be gone in a few days. I am here to finalize some personal business. Then I'm headed back to the North Country," Chris said, attempting to reassure the biker.

Rockhound nodded his approval, and the men peeled off, leaving Chris still sitting roadside, smoking his cigar. He watched as their red colors faded into the distance, then looked down, shaking his head. He crushed out his smoke and started up his own bike. He glanced back at the town one more time, then turned to head toward the FARM. When he passed by a sign to the left that said Old Federal Hwy, his mind started racing.

Why did I come back? he thought. What does all of this mean?

He silently searched his own thoughts for the answers but eventually thought, I don't know, but I have got to get out of here ASAP.

He had two more stops before going to Church.

Maybe then I can get some answers to this puzzle, he thought to himself.

Chapter 6

Ghost in the Moon

"Listen to me. All I know is what Sammy told me!" Bear, a tall, muscular, bald-headed man, shouted as he leaned his large arms on the bar top. "He said that Preach was back in town and that we have to all be at Chapel tonight at eighteen hundred hours."

His partner, Sack, sat there listening to both him and the TV screen above the bar.

"It looks like Domingo and all of the Brothers are coming in on this. They called a Council of Twelve," Bear said with a bit more excitement in his voice.

Sack now turned to pay more attention.

"Hell, they even called Marcus and Luke," Bear said, taking a swig of his beer and then setting it back down, taking a second to watch the expression on his partner's change. "This must be something big. Sammy told me to bring in the war wagon and to have Sissy and the girls ready to go."

"I don't like the way this is looking, Bro," Sack said as he lit a cigarette.

"I don't know, but he is riding solo. At least, he came into town solo. Our man in the department said that he had something to do with the armed robbery at the Kang. He also said that Preach stopped the Skullys single-handedly or something," Bear said.

"I just don't like this. It could shake things up," Sack commented.

"It'll be okay. Preach is one of us," Bear said.

They both took a shot of whiskey that the female bartender had poured, then looked up to see the scores on the screen.

"Why do they call him 'Preach,' anyway?" the girl behind the bar asked.

42

Bear took another sip of his beer and began to explain, saying, "Rumor has it that just before he kills, he quotes some old hocus-pocus lines from the Bible or something. It's like he gives you your final rights before you die."

The girl looked at the two men, her mouth hanging open.

"Are you for real?" she said with a mixture of intrigue and fear.

"He used to be an enforcer. It's been said that before he fires a shot, he says a prayer. If he were beside you as you died, he would send you to hell. He used to weird me out with all his Jesus stuff," Bear said. "I heard he went off to die after his mama passed away. He sort of snapped or something. He just vanished, like a ghost in the moon."

The doors to the clubhouse opened. Bear, Sack, and the bartender all turned to see Doc, Sammy, Cowboy, Dutch, and several others file in. They were followed by several women.

"What do you mean? How can nobody know?" Doc asked Sammy as they drew closer to the bar.

"You guys are worried about nothing. Preach is only here for a few days, and then he will disappear again. Let's just see how it plays out at Church," Sammy said, trying to calm down the overly excited group. "Has JT gotten here yet?"

No one could respond.

Chapter 7

Stone Walls

Chris rode along the backroads that led into Dodson Forest. He scanned the sky through the trees. It was like seeing the blueness of an ocean high above. Not a single cloud could be seen. The road was shaded by the trees, and the sun peeked through with its warm rays from time to time, kissing his cheeks. To both sides of the road, Irish roses grew wild, scenting the air. Up ahead was the river. Fresh water came down from the mountain streams and went into the rushing currents of the snake-like river, and the sound of the water helped calm his nerves. Large stone walls were on both sides of the bridge, separating the road from the water.

The sights and sounds turned his thoughts to a friendship from long ago, and his mind flashed back.

***

"Get down, you idiot!" the voice of a soldier behind him commanded. "You're gonna get yourself killed!"

"I can't leave them out there, Will!" Chris yelled back as he fired two rounds toward the top of the building where the shots were being unloaded.

Firing two more rounds, he darted out into the street, AK fire following his footsteps. He ducked in behind the remains of an old truck, took a deep breath, and quickly looked across the street. Will was returning fire to cover him, so he reacted to his cover and once again raced across the street and into the building on the other side. He knew that he was breaking protocol by leaving his battle buddy behind in the street, and he was breaking it even more so now that he was entering a hostile environment with untold numbers of "unfriendlies."

"Sergeant Caldwell! Do not enter that building!" the voice of the radio operator commanded through his earbuds. "There are at least ten to twelve hostiles inside! I repeat, do not continue forward!"

Chris stopped long enough to check his magazines and mentally count his remaining rounds. He felt his gear.

I have twenty-plus rounds left. My sidearm is empty, he thought to himself.

"Sergeant!" the voice screamed.

"Listen, I will not leave my men out there to get picked off one by one. I have several pinned down out there. I have wounded and casualties. If I don't go in, we are all dead," he said into his battle mic. "I'm not sending their mamas bodies. I'm getting us home!"

"Sergeant—"

With that, Chris pulled the earpiece out of his ear and removed his pack. He double-checked his magazine and looked up just in time to see Will Stone rush into the room where he was crouched.

"You are one crazy SOB!" Will said as he came in beside Chris.

"Give me a mag and watch that door at our six!" Chris said as he reached out his hand.

"All I have is in the fourteen and in my SIG!"

Chris looked up the stairs and gave it a quick thought.

"Give me the SIG," he said as he pulled out two percussion grenades. "No matter what, do not leave this room, Will!" He looked at Will and then back up the stairs. "I'll see you when we get there, bro!"

He headed up the stairs. His M14 was ready to fire, the SIG tucked into his rear waistband.

***

The sound of laughter coming from the trailhead woke Chris up from his daydreaming. He now sat on the stone walls that surrounded the edge of the walking path that ran north to south just east of the river. The children were racing and playing some form of tag, catching his attention. He began to smile as he saw the happiness in their spirits, their joyful playfulness. It had been such a long time since he had felt any type of peace, much less happiness. The world around him seemed to continuously drag him back into the dark corners of resentment and regret. But right now, watching the boys play together seemed like a magical fairytale moment.

The young mother who was with the boys noticed him and seemed to suddenly be alarmed, probably because he was dressed in black. He was aware of his vile appearance and tried his best to smile and make the woman see that he was harmless. But at this moment, all she saw was a biker, a monster wearing leather and denim. His long hair was pulled back and inside a skullcap, and though his beard was now cleaned up and somewhat well kept, as far as she knew, this beast was dangerous.

"Boys, stay back from the nice man, please," she said with a fake smile and focused eyes.

The boys looked up and immediately went back toward their mother.

Chris could see things from both his point of view and the mother's. He hoped, at this moment, those kids would never know what it felt like to be in his boots. He was a father. He would protect his kids with his last breath, just as his parents would have for him and his younger brother. He knew well her reasons to be protective. But he still couldn't help but feel hurt. She had no idea who he was or what he was capable of in any situation.

He smiled again, stood up, and walked away from them. There was an overlook that had a grand view of the waterfalls. He leaned against the railing and drifted back into his memories again.

She has no idea just how much of a monster I really am, he thought to himself.

His emotions were running to and fro, going from hurt to anger to sympathy and back again. He closed his eyes and listened to the sound of the river, the sound of cars driving across the bridge, and the sound of the children playing. It all made his mind return to dark thoughts. His heart had become stone cold, like the walls of rock lining the trail. He was hardened. Cold. Was it too late? Would the coldness in him force him further into darkness? He looked at his hands. They had spilt the blood of men. He had taken life. Maybe the woman's thoughts of him were correct. Maybe he was a monster. Less than human. Right now, that was exactly how he felt as he looked at his hands and then plunged them into the river water below.

***

He made his way up three flights of stairs. He had at least three more to go. He had not seen anyone yet, but he could hear the sound of Will's weapon being fired below him as well as the sound of a high-caliber rifle from somewhere up above him. He approached the next level of stairs cautiously. When he started to make the turn, machine-gun rounds sprayed the wall behind him. He could hear the men screaming at one another and at him in Arabic. He took one of the percussion grenades out of his belt and pulled the pin, tossing it down the hallway. He could hear the panic in their voices rise as the PG went off. He rushed down the hall and heard bodies hit the floor.

"One, two, buckle my shoe," he counted. "Three, four, bodies on the floor."

A fifth man popped his head out of the door up ahead. Chris reacted and placed a single round in his left eye socket.

"Five dead."

As he reached the door where the fifth man lay, he could hear gunfire behind him, the bullets hitting just left of where he stood. He spun around to return fire at the men headed toward him. The bodies, as if in slow motion, crumpled to the ground as he started to fire.

Will Stone stood in the doorway of the stairs Chris had come up. He gave Will a double look.

"Six, seven, bad guys down," he counted as he looked at Will and then at the bodies lying between them.

"I'm eighty-six!" Will called out, telling him he was out of ammunition.

"Will, find a spot and stay put!"

He passed Will to race up the stairs. He checked his M14 magazine.

Empty, he thought to himself as he reached behind him to retrieve the 9mm SIG Sauer.

"'The Lord is my Shepherd...'" he began to whisper under his breath.

He took position and checked the doorknob to see if the floor was clear. It opened into another hallway. He knew that he had to clear the floor before heading any farther up. He couldn't afford to pin himself in from all sides. One clip was all he had left. He had to make this count. He turned and moved out the door, away from any worthy cover. His weapon ready, he made his way down the hallway, opening one door at a time. When he opened the fourth door, he found two women on the floor in the far corner of the room. They were cuddled together, two children hiding behind them. A fallen soldier lay on the floor in front of the window. A second man was hanging halfway out the window that overlooked the street.

"Eight, nine, less rugs to clean," he calculated.

Looking at the ladies, he motioned for them to stay quiet and still as he headed toward the next three doors. They were all locked. It was too risky to try and kick them open to clear the rooms, so he headed back up the hallway and moved toward the stairs. Just as he reached the stairway door, a bullet missed his head by an inch. He dropped to a knee to return fire. An uncontrolled flurry of bullets arrived from one of the rooms. A soldier got caught in its spray, falling head-first into the hallway.

"Ten."

He gave the scared woman a thankful nod and headed up.

"'...though I walk through the valley of the shadow of death, I will fear no evil...'" he whispered. "Last floor, Chris. Last floor."

He slowly twisted the doorknob. It opened, and he cleared the hallway before going out.

Empty, he thought as he made his way down the hall.

He could hear the sniper gunfire from where he was.

Possibly three to four on the right, he thought.

He was out of options. He only had Will's SIG and his two tactical blades on his sides. As he got closer to the noise of gunfire, he heard footsteps coming fast. He backed off into an open room and placed the sidearm in his waistband. He drew one of his blades. His only chance of taking out the sniper would be to take him by surprise. If he fired the SIG, it would alert anyone in the rooms beyond where he stood. He watched from the darkness of his hiding place as two armed men hustled by him.

He jumped out behind the men, making his first cut to the rear man's right arm. As he reacted to the slice, Chris reached around him, grabbing the man's jacket's right-side lapel. He made his second cut along the right armpit, spinning him around to the left to use him as a shield. The second man, surprised by the sudden movement behind him, turned just in time to see Chris skillfully make the final cut across the man's left carotid artery. The lifeless man dropped to the floor.

The man standing raised his weapon to fire, but Chris kicked him solidly in the chest, causing him to drop the Russian-made weapon to the carpet. The soldier tried to regroup and sprung at Chris. The two men swapped blows, each blocking and returning attacks. Chris still had his blade, so he tried to slice at his foe with each movement. The soldier caught Chris with a solid right punch, sending him backward and to the floor. Chris was hurt and used his forearm to wipe away the blood pouring from his face, the blade still in his hand and a large smile on his face. He looked at his overconfident foe. The man rushed in with a big overhand right. Chris side-stepped, catching his right wrist and turning sharply to his left, sending the man flying through the air as his wrist, elbow, and shoulder all crumbled and snapped in unison. Chris made his final cut, turning the man into a lifeless heap.

Chris reached behind him and grabbed his SIG with his right hand, and after wiping the blood from his blade on the dead soldier's jacket, he secured it back in its sheath. Looking back up the hallway again, he made his way toward the sniper's lair.

"Eleven, twelve," he said, continuing his body count as he stepped over them.

He paused only long enough to breathe.

"His rod and His staff, they comfort me," he whispered as he kicked open the door, rushing mindlessly into the pitch-black room.

He fired a single round at the ceiling to create just enough light so he could find his target, then fired two final rounds at the sniper standing at the far-left window. He heard the body drop to the floor as he went down on a single knee, ready to shoot again if necessary. After a few moments with no movement in the room, he reached into his gear pocket and retrieved his lantern.

"Thirteen, fourteen," he whispered, looking down at the dead sniper.

He made his way to the window and pulled back the blinds so he could glance down. Four men lay dead in the street below. Good men. Friends. Brothers. At his own feet, along with the man he killed, he saw the bodies of a single sniper and a spotter, both with head wounds courtesy of Will's SIG. Chris used his boot to roll the sniper over.

"A female… My God," he said as he closed her eyes.

He left the room and headed back downstairs, where he found Will. The two acknowledged one another and headed out the door leading into the street. The other rangers came out to clear the road in all directions. They all looked at one another and then at their fallen Brothers. A tear fell from Chris's eye as he bowed his head in silence.

***

"The devil you know is better than the devil you don't," he said as his mind once again came out of the daydream.

Maybe I am a monster, he thought.

He looked at the family eating their meal together on the steps of the bridge.

"The devil you know…" he whispered as he hung his head.

He made his way back to his bike, which he had left in the gravel parking area of the park. He followed the set of stone walls, thinking about the cold hardness he had become.

There was some truth in his words, he thought as he remembered what Ricky Saunders had said back in town.

"Forgotten."

The bike let out an evil-sounding growl as he hit the ignition switch. Pulling back out onto the mountain road, he twisted the throttle, sped up, and crossed over Three Mile Creek Bridge. As he drove, he found himself in a mental battlefield. Chess in his mind. He had to find his way to checkmate soon. Why was he back here again? The note had gotten his attention, but it made no more sense now than it had when he found it. Come Home. That's all it had said. But it wasn't the words themselves. It was that red ink.

Chapter 8

T.R.O.U.B.L.E

The mountain road slowly began turning back into a double-lane road as Chris neared town. He knew that he only had a short time left before 18:00. He knew that he had no choice but to be at Chapel. This, more than anything else, was not optional. He turned onto Main Street, made his way to Tunnel Hill Road, and then drove down to Mason Trail. He could see the buildings up ahead. Two- and three-story old-style structures. If anyone were to ask, he would compare this place to the play Our Town, or maybe even to Mayberry, North Carolina from The Andy Griffith Show.

Just as he crossed over Prinkle Street, there she was. She literally took his breath from him.

"I don't have time for this," he said to himself as he slowed down his bike, watching her cross the street behind him.

Cursing himself under his breath, he put on his right turn signal and pulled into the parking lot, turning around to go back up the street, where the building she had just entered was. He backed his bike into a spot and looked at his reflection in the rearview mirror of his bike. He took off his helmet, pulled his hair back into a tight bun, and then hid it inside his skullcap beanie. He ran his hands down his black and white beard the best he could and got off his motorcycle. He looked up at the sign on the brick building. Goodson's Drugstore. It was one of those old-time town chemists, with the large Rx sign outside the doors.

He checked himself once again in the window's reflection before walking inside. The clerk at the front of the store welcomed him without even looking up, and he made his way down the center aisle. His eyes scanned the interior. The chemist counter was at the end of the aisle, and he saw a number of people standing in line. She was not among them, so he turned to check in the other direction. The aisles all had signs with numbers and content printed on them: 4, Cold and Flu; 5, Vitamins; 6, Tissue; and 7, Stationery and School Supplies.

Then he found her… She was in 8, Books and Magazines and Literature. He walked by the aisle and made his way down the next one: 9, Cosmetics and Beauty. He couldn't help but laugh to himself as he realized what aisle he was on, and an older woman looked up, noticing him coming down the row. He was watching the girl in aisle eight as he made his way down. He smiled as he listened to her sing the lyrics to the music coming from the store's sound system. He doubled back up her aisle, stopping just short of her at the magazines. He stood there listening to her hum along as she read through the item in her hands. She had not taken notice of him as far as he could tell, but it really didn't matter.

"Excuse me. Can you hand me a copy of that Cosmopolitan?" he asked, chuckling as he spoke.

She looked up and over at him, rolled her eyes, and looked down at the rack in front of her.

"You want a Cosmo?" she said as she studied him, looking his black boots, his bearded face, his black knitted skullcap, his black leather cut, the silver chain connected to his wallet, and the white and black handkerchief flag in his rear pocket.

"Well, sure. That's a great read," he said, trying to appear completely serious. "A guy can learn all kinds of interesting stuff in a Cosmo."

Once again, she rolled her eyes at him. The last thing in the world that she needed, or wanted, in her life was a biker. As far as she was concerned, she wasn't even remotely interested in a man at all.

"I'm not interested," she said as she hit him in the chest with the magazine.

"All I wanted was the magazine. Thanks for the help," he said as he turned to walk away.

He never looked back, but he felt her eyes on him as he went to the counter. He paid for his Cosmo and made his exit.

A smile came to her face. A beautiful smile it was. It was the kind of smile that could turn a fierce storm into a rainbow.

"TROUBLE," she whispered to herself as she picked up her own copy of Cosmopolitan.

She then watched him straddle his bike and pull off.

"MINE," he quietly said to himself as he headed back up the street.

Chapter 9

Change on the Horizon

One more stop before Chapel. Chris was running behind schedule, but this stop was of grave importance. As he continued to ride, he started correcting himself in his head. More mind chess.

You went through all of that, and you didn't so much as get her number. Not even her name. Idiot. What is wrong with you?

He watched a black Harbinger fly up ahead in the reddening sky.

I'll see her again. Patient birds get their rewards.

He made his turn onto Roper Church Road, slowing down to make another turn into a driveway just beyond the church. The mailbox read Marcus O' Kelly. He pulled up to the front of the ranch-style home and turned off his engine. As he made his way up the walk to the porch, a familiar voice came from the garage on the side.

"I ain't buying whatever you're selling."

Chris turned to see Marcus, the older man come out of the garage, wiping his hands with an old rag.

"Well, you couldn't afford it anyway," he chimed back as he made his way toward him.

As they drew closer to each other, Marcus reached out, pulling Chris toward him in a warm embrace, pulling away only to take a good, long look at the man in front of him.

"You need a haircut and a good shave, lad," he joked in his thick Irish accent. "You look older than me, lad, and I was with Moses when he waved that stick and God parted the Red Sea."

The two men laughed together.

Marcus took Chris by the arm, and they headed for the house. Just as they reached the porch, a pretty older lady opened the screen door.

"Christopher Caldwell! Oh my dear Jesus," she said as Chris looked at her and then back at Marcus.

"Ms. Ruth?" he said, shocked, as he moved toward her.

"Don't use my name in vain, boy. Give me a hug," she said as she embraced him.

"Um, Ms. Ruth?" he repeated again.

Marcus spoke up before she could and said with a smile, "We tied the knot last spring, Preach. She made me honest."

All Chris could do was look at both of them as Marcus pulled her into his arms.

"Well, he made me wait..." she joked back.

She kissed Marcus on the cheek and excused herself to the house as they sat down in the twin porch rockers.

"A lot's changed, my boy," Marcus said, lovingly stealing a glance at his bride as she walked into the kitchen.

"Well, I can see that. You coming to Church tonight?" Chris said in a whisper.

"Yeah, laddy, I'll be there. Not that it's my heart's desire. But I'm not at liberty to refuse," he said as he looked back at Chris. "And you don't have to whisper. I don't keep secrets from my love."

Chris looked at his old friend and then into the house at Mrs. Ruth. Then he looked back out at the garage.

"What's on the rack?" he asked, trying to change the subject.

"It's a sixty-eight Pan. I found it at the old house. I've rebuilt most of it. Trying to finish her up. I don't really know what I'll do when it's ready. But you know me. I like to get my hands dirty," Marcus said, studying Chris's body language.

Chris started to say something, but Mrs. Ruth came back out with two fresh iced teas. They both stood as she came to them.

"Thank you, Mrs. Ruth," Chris said as he took his glass.

"Yes, thank you, my love," Marcus added.

"See, Christopher. That's how he reeled me onto his boat." She smiled. "Have you been down to the river to see your daddy?"

She put her hands on her hips, looking as if she could read his soul.

"No, ma'am. I haven't had time yet," he said, and she popped him on the head.

"You be sure that you make time, boy!" she barked. Quietly, she added, "He needs his sons."

"He has Daniel," Chris replied.

"Boy! Don't make me hit you again. Your daddy needs both of you, not just Daniel," she said as she raised her hand to pop him again. "Family endures, Christopher."

Chris stood back, knowing his next words could get him hit again. He looked at Marcus for help. None came.

"My family died three years ago."

"Ruthie, go back inside before I have to call a coroner for our young friend," Marcus said, laughing.

Chris looked at them, then sat down beside Marcus as he watched Mrs. Ruth go back inside.

"You can't win against a lass, Preach. It's a lose-lose," Marcus said, taking a sip of his tea. "Besides, she is right. And you are wrong. You have family. I'm your family. The Lost Boys are your Family," he said sternly. "But most importantly, your father and your brother are your blood. They need you."

Chris looked back out at the garage and said, "We had a lot of fun in that box. I think about all the hard cases you helped me with."

Marcus just sat back in his rocker, listening.

"Yeah, lad. We did. We will again," he said, watching Chris.

Chris looked at him, gave an awkward smile, and said, "I just wanted to drop by to see you before Church. I'm not sure how things will go tonight, but I'll be riding out in few days."

"I'll be right there beside you, Preach. Why are you home, anyway?"

Chris reached into his pocket and pulled out the note.

"I got this back in Murphy," he said as he handed it to Marcus.

Marcus looked at the note and handed it back.

"Any idea what it means?"

"No, sir. I was hoping maybe you could help me figure it out."

Marcus said nothing but leaned over to pick up an apple seed on the porch.

"It looks like Mama's handwriting, but how can that be possible?" Chris asked as he looked at the red ink and then put the note away.

"What's impossible for man—" Marcus started to say, but Chris quickly interrupted.

"I don't want to hear empty words from a God who forgot me."

"Nothing—absolutely nothing—is impossible for God," Marcus said strongly. "I know that you are still hurting, but—"

Chris didn't let him finish. He got up from his rocker and headed down the steps. He turned around before he got to his bike and looked back at Marcus.

"You are not forgotten, Preach. Not by your Family. And absolutely not by your heavenly Father," Marcus said sternly, then turned to go back inside the house.

Mrs. Ruth, standing off in the distance, watched from the kitchen.

"Hey!" Marcus yelled out to him.

Chris looked back again as he straddled his saddle.

"I'll see you when we get there," Marcus concluded and walked inside to embrace his concerned wife.

Chris cranked up to leave. He looked back at the house, then at the garage. Above it, three flags flew. Glory. Old Yellow. The Jolly Roger.

"What in the hell is going on?" he cursed as he rode off.

17:45. He had fifteen minutes to get to Chapel. This day was turning into an uncomfortable mess.

"What else?" he wondered.

Chapter 10

El Regreso del Predicador

Not a single vehicle seemed to be on the road now, which was not normal considering that it was 18:00 on a weekday. There was an occasional car or truck here and there, but nothing much to note. Traffic should be congesting the main road as everyone tried to get home. Not today.

Chris was headed back to the FARM. As he got closer, he could see two riders parked to the side of Three Mile Creek Bridge. He knew that one was a lookout scout, and the second rider had been given the responsibility of being his ghost escort to Church. It wasn't because they were concerned about him not showing up; it was security protocol that had been designed by him. They were following it to the letter. The rules of the club clearly stated that no one was to ride solo while wearing colors, although he had been on his own up until now.

Just as he assumed, one of the riders stayed behind, and the other pulled in beside him on his left to ghost the ride in. The ghost was an exceptionally large and muscular man. His arms were inked on both sides, and he flew his colors proudly. He was covered with a black and white bandana, protective glasses, leather gloves, and his turtle-shell-style helmet, and he was wearing leathers to protect from the road's elements. He gave Chris a hand greeting common to bikers and pulled up ahead to lead the way.

There would be high security tonight, as all twelve of the Council of Twelve would be assembled together in one location.

As they approached the FARM's gates, the greeting squad moved into position like a finely tuned clock, each radioing to the other that the guests were arriving. A man began opening the large front gate so that it was fully open. Two other sentry guards could be seen on the rooftops, most likely set up to be snipers. There were only two SUVs parked in the business portion of the compound. Eight black Harleys sat facing the main road. The position and number of them held a hidden message for any Lost Boys riding in unexpectedly.

Chris and his ghost escort drove through the gate. The two sentry guards up above offered a subtle hand greeting to Chris and then moved quickly back into position. The ground crew went into action, shutting the gates behind them as they cleared the fence line.

The interior courts of the compound were packed. His best estimate was that probably three to four hundred bikes of every shape, color, and size filled the normally massive-looking courtyard. The bikes were all American-made and formed row after row of steel and rubber. Everyone stopped what they were doing, heads turning as the two riders rode by them.

Chris could not imagine a valid reason for such a large turnout. Funerals. Weddings. They had big turnouts. To some, this could be the same as a funeral. Charity rides. Disassociation rites. Those called for such a large number of Lost Boys. He wasn't taking part in any of those four situations, unless, of course, the Brothers had decided to remove Chris from the club. In that case, the ceremony would not be favorable. Fire or steel.

He watched the actions of the men moving around him. Church itself could only hold twelve at the table and six along the walls, as that was part of club ritual. The clubhouse could host seventy to eighty comfortably. But the number in the courtyard alone was almost impossible.

As they kicked down in their prearranged positions, he noticed the movement of a dozen sentries on the rooftops. Silence filled the courtyard. Dead silence. Every eye in the yard was locked in on Chris as he stepped off of his saddle. He slowly took off his helmet and placed it on his forward controls. Three things were for certain:

1. Each man in the yard was a dangerous animal. Almost all of them would be armed with a variety of sidearms of various caliber.

2. Although he was also armed, they would seize his weapons, all the way down to the red Swiss Army knife in his jeans pocket, before he stepped into the clubhouse this time.

3. Regardless of the purpose or the outcome of this session of Church, they had all gathered tonight to party. Drugs, booze, women, and undoubtedly more than a handful of brawls would lay in the aftermath of this call to arms.

But why? What could be this paramount? Chris had not returned to stay. He was only back to find out the meaning of the red-inked note. The puzzle was getting larger.

The ghost escort had taken off his coverings, but he was facing away from Chris's position. His head was freshly shaven.

Chris scanned the yard. The menacing stares would have been enough to cause even the most courageous warrior to be nervous, but he did not fear death. He welcomed it. He had walked in its shadow. He had kicked its ass. He would face it again. With honor. He raised up his right fist, tapping his heart and raising it high again into the air. The crowd erupted in unison. One single voice coming from hundreds of bodies. Every fist followed Chris's example. They were all raised high.

"Aroo! Aroo! Aroo!" the multitude exploded in cheer.

He couldn't hold back his grin.

"Brothers..." he whispered to himself.

"BROTHERS!" the crowd roared as if on cue.

The ghost escort turned around to face Chris. As they locked eyes, Chris's smile grew larger. Mac, the large, bald rider, turned his face to the side, looking out toward the crowds, then looked back at Chris. A large scar ran down his face, starting above his right eye and going down his cheekbone to his chin. He spat brown goo from his mouth and made his way over to where Chris stood. They both removed their right riding glove and clasped arms.

"Welcome home, Brother," he said, looking at Chris and then back out at the crowd.

"Show off."

The two men embraced in a hug, and Chris responded, "I'll be gone soon enough, son. Don't worry."

"Not if I have any say," Mac fired back.

Chris just peered over at him as two sentries approached to wand him for recording devices and to take his weapons. In the distance, he could see several women making their way from the pub's rear doorway, carrying boxes of beer and bottles of Irish whiskey. A young man followed them and was wheeling a dolly transporting two large kegs. They made their way into the clubhouse.

The room was packed. Standing room only. Chris's senses caught the strong scent of loud reefer.

"Damn, Mac," Chris said in surprise. "How many Boys are here?" he asked.

The large man looked around the room and said, "Enough."

Chris looked around the room again. A game of nine ball was underway. Three groups of men were surrounded by dozens of barely dressed women, some playing darts, some simply watching their surroundings. The faces all seemed familiar. Lost Boys. Loyal Sisters. Hang arounds. As well as a half dozen probates working the bar, serving drinks as fast as they could.

"We added cameras to the courtyard, the rear decks, and the inside of this room. The only place not under surveillance is Church," Mac said, catching Chris up on surveillance improvements as they walked through the clubhouse.

"I see that," Chris offered as he watched and waited for Mac to continue.

"What have you been doing out there, Preach?" Mac said abruptly. "I came out to NC a few months back. I was looking for you." He leaned against the bar. "I called, but you never responded. I half expected to see you in PCB last spring. You became a shadow, a ghost. Right when I thought I'd found you...gone."

He sounded concerned, and Chris said, "I know, Mac. I'm sorry. I had to get away. I had to take myself as far away as I could for the sake of the Club. It was just too hard after Mama died. I was losing my grip fast."

"Sal!" Mac yelled at a bartender.

The probate working the bar came over to Mac. Seeing Chris, he stopped and pulled out a bottle of Jameson. He began to pour two tall drinks.

"Irish breakfast, right?" Sal said as he shoved the drinks in front of Mac and Chris.

The probate greeted Mac and took a long look at Chris. He knew better than to say anything out of the way, especially with the current Sergeant at Arms and the legendary Captain of the Guard standing in front of him. He was itching to say something, but he thought better of it and went about his duties instead.

"Rule number eight: Leave no room for excuses. Never say you're sorry," Mac said as he placed his empty glass on the bar top. "Isn't that the rule?" he said sarcastically.

Chris just looked at his friend, but he didn't respond. He finished his own drink quickly and continued studying the crowd. Sal began mixing two more drinks for Chris and Mac.

"Pour that crap out, probie!" Mac demanded.

Sal looked at the drinks he had already poured, knowing he had not messed up.

"Yes, sir," he answered.

"Two ounces of Jameson, one ounce of butterscotch Schnapps, ice, and orange juice. Idiot!" Mac barked, looking over at Chris with a grin.

It was the job and pleasure of any patched-in Brother to make a probate's life miserable. It would make them or break them. Either way, it was the only path to becoming patched.

Chris didn't show any emotion. He just went with the way things were.

Sal mixed two more drinks, stepping away to empty the other drinks.

"Hey! Your mouth is the sink tonight! All mistakes, you drink!" Mac playfully picked at Sal.

At that, Sal knew he was in for a long night, a very intoxicated one.

Mac stepped toward the mini stage of the clubhouse.

"Listen up! This here is one of the men that we owe and have to thank for all of this!" he said, making a large motion with his arms, pointing around the room but also meaning everything about the FARM and the Lost Boys as a whole.

"Brother, we salute you," he said, toasting Chris with his glass.

Chris looked around the room and watched as every glass, bottle of beer, whiskey bottle, and fist raised toward him. He tapped his glass against Mac's as the clubhouse roared once more in unison.

"Aroo! Aroo! Aroo!" they cheered.

Chris drank down his drink and slammed it back on the bar top. He raised his right fist in the air again.

"Forever endures!" he yelled as the room erupted, the sounds echoing throughout the room.

"BROTHERS!" the room, including Chris, chanted.

They all took drinks of their own and then went back to what they were doing.

The comradeship. The Brotherhood. The Lost Boys MC. That was what it was about. FAMILY.

"Hey, sexy man," said a soft voice beside Chris.

"Marla, right?" he asked.

"You can call me whatever you want, but yes, Marla is my name," she said as she rubbed his arm with one hand, his chest with the other.

Chris looked at Mac, who only offered him a sly grin in return, patting him on the back as Marla stepped in closer, putting her arms around Chris's neck. He didn't resist her, instead pulling her into him. She kissed his lips softly and then shot him a sweet smile.

"When Church is over, you owe me a dance, Preach," she whispered in his ear.

He smiled and nodded.

She turned away, walking off, but stopped short to look back at him. She was wearing cowboy boots, short cutoff shorts, and a white shirt that was tied at her belly. She was sexy, there was no denying that. She knew it. She also knew her place. It was more than just a game to her, though. She had a plan. She was what the club called a "Loyal Sister," but her ultimate goal was to become someone's Lady. The higher the rank, the better. If she got lucky enough for it to be someone as popular and respected as Chris, that would be perfect.

Chris knew the rules of the game, too. He knew that if he wanted her, she was his for as long as he wanted, even if only for a few hours. He was also very aware of what she really wanted and knew that he could never give it to her. He had given up that pursuit long ago, after the breakup between him and his yet-to-be born baby girl's mama. He had sworn that he would never again open up his heart to another person.

Chapter 11

church

"Let's go, Boys!" said a demanding voice from the side of the bar where they had been standing. "Church time!"

From somewhere outside the clubhouse, the sound of a bag piper's song could be heard, calling in the Council of Twelve. Mac, Chris, and several others stepped away from what they were doing to make their way into a large conference-style room. A large round table sat in the center of the room. It was made from heavily stained cedar. In the center of it was an engraved raven that was perched upon a skull, the words LOST BOYS engraved across the top. One large chair and eleven smaller ones circled the table. There were men already sitting in some of the chairs saved for positions of rank. Six patched officers. Four veteran patches. The Vice President. The club presidential chair. Each seat had filled up except for the Captain of the Guard's seat. The VP's seat and the presidential chair remained vacant.

Chris looked around the room at his Brothers. Each one of them wore a chest patch that said Man of Valor. They had all earned the right to wear that tag by "bleeding" for the club.

He looked at the decor of the room. The walls were covered with picture frames. One wall held the flags. Nothing had changed about this room except for the few new butts in the royal seats. He remained standing along the wall.

The door to another room opened dramatically as the club's President and VP, JT Pain and Jorge "Flako" Santiago, took their places at the table. Thor, the current Captain of the Guard, also called the club's "Cappo" stood reluctantly behind his chair.

"This is your chair, Preach," Thor said to Chris with respect.

"I'm good, my friend. That's your chair now. Not mine," Chris said, gesturing for the huge red-bearded man to sit.

"Take your seat, Preach!" This time, it was JT making the command.

Chris walked over to the table and placed both fists solidly on the beautiful cedar table. He looked at the artwork of the club, the Harbinger and skull, that was carved into the dark wood. He slowly looked around the Church room.

"This is a sacred hall. This table represents Brotherhood, loyalty, and Family." He spoke with respect for the men sitting and those standing. "I said that I am fine standing. That chair belongs to Thor now."

JT was visibly enraged by the rejection.

"I said, sit!" he screamed as he slammed his fist on the table's surface.

Everyone in the room watched both men intently.

Chris looked right through JT and said as respectfully as possible, "I didn't come here to fight. I didn't come to start a war. Or to argue. Or to change anything from how things are now. But... if I were sitting at this table as a voice, I'd be in your chair, not at third."

He had made his speech with conviction, never taking his eyes off of JT.

"Is that right?" JT responded.

He was obviously angered that Chris had suggested that he didn't belong in his chair, but also because he dared to speak in such a tone to him. After all, he was "the President" of Lost Boys MC.

The room was full of tension. No one knew what would happen next.

Flako finally broke the silence and said, "We have business to cover, my Brothers. Preach, you know you are welcome to sit, stand, or whatever you want to do." He was clearly trying to ease the room's temperament. "Part of this is about you being back, and you have partly answered that."

Chris stepped back and leaned back on the wall, JT still staring intensely at him. JT finally took his gavel and gave the table three loud strikes. Every man in the room began repeating the Lost Boys code.

"We are the Brotherhood of Lost Boys. Come as one. In unity, we stand. In division, we fall. We stand ready to defend our place in history. Our word is our bond. Our bond is our life. Only death can separate our covenant."

Chris couldn't help but wonder to himself if JT even understood that oath. When the men finished their covenant, Flako began to speak again, JT still looking at Chris, Chris comfortably returning the stare.

"First order of business. Preach, what is your position among us? Do we need to vote?"

Flako looked around the room. Chris did the same.

"Listen to me, Brothers," Chris began. "As I said, I am not here to change things. I am not here to take command. JT is your alpha. I came back to solve a private puzzle." He pulled the note from his cut. "I just want to know what this means," he said, showing the room the wrinkled brown paper in his hand. "I want to know where it came from. I am and always will be a Lost Boy, but you, Brothers, are doing just fine without me."

He finished and stepped back. Several of the men started talking at once. Some were now insisting that Chris shouldn't even be in Church since he was not an officer, while others spoke up in his defense, saying that he had come to be part of their world again.

Mac was seated at the table, looking up at Chris, and said, "I'll follow you to hell, Brother. You know that. I'll be right there beside you trying to bootleg ice water. But we need to know where you stand."

Several others nodded in agreement.

A hand rested on Chris's shoulder. It was Marcus. Standing beside him were Luke and Chigger, three of the "Original Eight."

"How can we help you, Preach?" Marcus said as Chris looked back at him, then back at the room of rugged bikers.

"All that I need is time to figure this out," he offered as he lowered his head. "Then I'm gone."

He and JT made eye contact again.

"Okay then. Do what you need to do. You have the Lost Boys behind you," Marcus answered.

Everyone in the room, except JT, nodded in agreement, and JT hit the table for order.

"Fine, let's talk about the trucks," he said, trying to move on.

Church went on for another hour or so as they discussed club business, including the transportation of weapons and drugs to and from Mexico. The club had taken on new ventures in Chris's absence. It was no longer just money and greed. Now they were dealing with stolen military weapons. Sexual slave trafficking. Extortion of local businesses. Chris loved the original concepts: Brotherhood, loyalty, and Family. But something in him was now repulsed by what the club had become. He could care less about this new way. His focus was on solving the puzzle and leaving Alabama once again. The sooner, the better.

Chapter 12

Crimson Bones

"I don't care why he is back!" the drunk man yelled as he threw his half-empty beer bottle against the wall of the Skulls clubhouse. "Right now, for all we know, that psychopath could be working out a strategy to wipe us out." There was sincere concern in his voice. "I didn't work this hard for the last two years just to let it all blow up in my face."

Rockhound sat back in his chair and watched his VP rage.

"Tony, I know Preach. I've known him our whole lives. One thing I can promise you is that he hasn't come back to eliminate the Skulls," Rockhound said, trying to reassure his upset Brother. "In a few more days, he will vanish back into whatever hole he came from. We will be back ahead of schedule. LBMC will be dead, just like its heritage." He leaned over the table toward Tony and said, "If he isn't gone by Monday, I'll personally take care of the problem."

They looked at one another intently. Tony had calmed down a little.

"Have you spoken to Cruz?" he asked as he opened another beer and sipped the cold brew. "What's his stand?"

Rockhound sat back in his chair again and folded his arms as he looked at his intoxicated Brother.

"They are just waiting for my call," he said firmly. "The Thirteens are looking for their crates on Sunday. They have our powder."

"All that we have to do is survive until then," Tony said, staring at the brown bottle in his fist.

"All we have to do is follow the plan, Tony. That's it."

Rockhound was growing impatient with Tony. He took a sip of his own drink, then looked at his nervous friend.

"The Butcher has already been paid. One call, and he will go to work," he said with confidence.

"Rock, we both know what Preach is capable of. I want him gone! Now!" Tony thundered, standing up and slamming the door behind him as he left the room.

Immediately, the door opened up again as two young men walked inside.

"What gives, Pop? Everything cool?" Ricky, Rockhound's son, asked as he looked out the door, watching Tony knock over several chairs as he stormed through the clubhouse common area.

"Yeah, it's all good," Rockhound said as he also watched his friend. "Get some of the boys to put a little pressure on our friend Preach. But not too much, Ricky. You have to be careful. That man doesn't have a soul." There was concern in his voice. "Rick, he will kill the lot of you and not flinch. Are we clear?"

"No problem, Pop. Consider it done," Ricky said as he looked at his companion, who was standing beside him. He grabbed his friend's injured shoulder and said, "Consider it payback time."

"Son, pressure. Don't underestimate that man. I don't want to bury you beside your silly pals," Rockhound warned as he took another sip of his drink.

He lit a cigarette and turned his attention back to the dozens of screens, each one with different images on them. Some showed hotel beds that were occupied by prostitutes and their clients. Another focused on a room full of naked women bagging up methamphetamine. Other screens played sports programs.

Ricky winked at his pal, rolled his eyes at his dad, and motioned for them to exit the room.

"Rick! Follow orders, son," Rockhound said as the two young men left.

Ricky and his pal gathered up a group of men and sat down at a table in the corner of the clubhouse common to make plans. Ricky's cell phone started buzzing, and he stood up and walked away to answer the call.

"What's up?" he said into the phone, looking around to see if anyone was paying attention. "You said that you would handle this. Handle it! Whatever you have to do, just do it. We are running out of time." He was beginning to grow red-faced as he got more and more irritated. "Are we clear? Just handle it, dammit! This is too important."

With that, he hung up and went back over to his Brothers, flashing a fake smile at them as he sat back down.

Chapter 13

Ultimatums

After the Council of Twelve concluded Church, one by one the members walked out, leaving Chris, Marcus, Luke, and JT behind.

JT leaned forward in his seat, took a long, hard look at the men standing in front of him, and said, "I should kill you where you stand, Preach. Why are you really back? No BS. I want the truth."

Chris looked at the three men in the room. He gritted his teeth. His fists began to tighten. The man he had once been known to be would have taken up JT's challenge. However, right now, all he really wanted to do was figure out who sent the message and what it meant, and just as soon as he had found out, he would go back to the Northlands. He would go back to being owner and CEO of Resurrection Security Services, and he would not have anything to do with this place.

"JT, I told you the truth," he said, looking at JT. "Not that I even had to do that. I don't owe you anything. But I actually believe in what the Lost Boys were founded upon." He began listing off one pillar at a time. "Loyalty. Respect. Honor. Brotherhood. Isn't that rule number two, JT? What happened to respecting the pillars of the club? My word is my bond, unlike others who are still in this club."

Chris was ready to explode, but he knew that there was no win here. If he called out the current president of Lost Boys MC, he would not make it off of the FARM's compound. He knew it.

JT looked hard at him and said, "Okay. You are right. I know what this club means to you." He paused. "What this chair means to you." He patted the leather throne and gave him a conceited and arrogant grin. "You have three days. After that, we need to figure some things out. You either take your place here, under my reign, or retire your patch and disappear again."

Chris looked at JT and then at his Brothers.

"It's that simple," JT said, grinning.

Chris took a deep breath and nodded his approval. He walked over to the cedar table and knocked twice while looking JT straight in the eyes, sending his own nonverbal message to everyone still in the room.

"Remember who I am."

He and his two Brothers left JT in the conference room alone.

Chapter 14

Behind the Eight

"I need a shot," Chris said as he grabbed his old friends' shoulders. "What will it be tonight, boys? Vodka or Home Country?"

Luke and Marcus laughed.

"I'll have the good stuff. A tall glass of Virginia sweet tea. But I'll buy you a drink," Marcus said as they walked together.

"I'll find you boys later. I've got to help set up," Luke said as he patted Chris's shoulder and nodded at Marcus.

Chris said goodbye to Luke and turned his attention back to Marcus, staring him down and saying, "You have got to be playing! What happened to my Irish shooter?"

Marcus just smiled and said, "I grew up, Preach."

Chris looked at his old friend and mentor as they walked out of the clubhouse and into the twilight air, making their way across the courtyard to the side door of The Belle. There were people everywhere. Inside and outside. He noticed that a band was playing on the stage outside, which was just to the rear of the clubhouse fence. Familiar faces and voices were all around him.

He knew that he was in the company of Brothers and friends, but something alerted his gut that he needed to be watchful. Something was not right. He didn't yet know what it was, but careful would be the approach.

They entered through the door of The Belle, which opened up into a room full of pool tables, dart boards, and people mingling. Most of them were Lost Boys, but there was a good mix of townies and civilians, too. Women in sexy attire were everywhere. Drunk and drugged-up men were working on their pickup games, both with pool and women.

Chris and Marcus headed past the crowd and moved toward the bar that was shaped like a large horseshoe. They both found a spot, and the bartender came to get their drink orders.

"Hey, guys. Y'all want the usual?"

Chris grinned and looked at his friend, then said, "Jameson for me, and a sweet tea for Gramps here."

Marcus smiled at the joke.

The bartender poured the shot of Irish whiskey and the sweet tea, and they tapped glasses without another word.

"Bobby, give me the bottle!" came a deep voice from behind them.

They both turned to look as the bartender pulled an unopened thirty-two-ounce platinum bottle of Jameson out from behind the bar.

"Put it on my tab, mate!" said Hank, a short-bearded man with an Irish swagger. Then he turned to Chris, giving him a sincere hug, and asked, "Brings ya to us, Brother?"

"I am just passing through, Hank. It's damn good to see you, though!" Chris said, looking at his old pal. "What brings you out?"

The three men settled in to talk.

"I'm singing up there in a bit, mate. Ya want to hear something special?" Hank asked as he pointed toward the small stage on the other side of the room.

"That's great, Brother. It's been a while since I heard you play."

Hank reached for the bottle on the bar, opened it, and took a big swig, then handed it to Chris.

"Drink up, Brother! Fine seeing ya!" he said as he grabbed Chris's shoulder, and then he returned to the band stage.

Chris looked at Marcus and held up the bottle with a devilish smile. Marcus raised his sweet tea and took a drink.

"I need to go, Preach. But let's get together before you leave." Marcus smiled and handed Chris a card with a number written on it. "That's my burner. Call it if you need anything."

With that, he walked toward the front door, Chris following behind him.

"Marcus, I've been here less than twenty-four hours. I'll be gone soon. It's been two years, man! What's up?"

"It's just not my scene anymore, lil Brother," Marcus said as he found his keys. "But seriously, let's get together before you leave. Ruth would love to see you."

He fumbled with his keys, not looking at Chris, and Chris could tell from his body language that he was wanting to say something but was hesitating.

"What is it, Marcus?" Chris asked, trying to get his old friend to engage.

"Have a good time tonight, Preach. The Boys are looking forward to spending time with their hero." Marcus looked up at Chris, his eyes almost watering. "Watch your six. Chris."

Marcus had rarely ever used his real name. Chris knew it was on purpose.

Marcus put his gloves on, followed by his helmet, then cranked up his Shovelhead and gave Chris a final nod as he pulled off, leaving Chris standing alone on the curb, whiskey bottle clenched in his right hand.

He turned to go back inside. The bouncer opened the door for him to enter, but just as he started to go inside, he took one more look at the main road. Marcus was no longer in sight, but he could still hear the growl of his hog in the distance. He raised the bottle to his lips and took in a massive gulp, the brown liquid burning his throat, then noticed a group of people walking up the hill toward him and the bouncer.

"Townies…" he joked under his breath.

At the end of the line of people, he caught a glimpse of a familiar face. He couldn't quite make her out at first. She was walking and reading a text on her cell phone. She looked up and smiled at one of the friends walking with her. Her smile. It was as much in her eyes as it was on her lips.

Beautiful… he thought.

It was her. The girl from earlier that afternoon.

He looked at the bouncer standing beside him and grinned as he handed him his bottle of whiskey.

"I'll help ya card a few of these townies."

The bouncer was okay with that because he knew the person standing beside him was not just a drunk biker. This was the former Lost Boys Cappo.

As she got closer to the door, all Chris could think about was the angelic sparkle in her brown eyes. She was special. He didn't know what it was, but it was not normal. She was unique.

"Good evening, ma'am," he said, giving her a slick grin as she got to him. "ID, please."

Up until this point, she hadn't looked up at Chris, but when she handed him her license and looked up at him, she seemed to recognize him immediately from their encounter earlier at the magazine rack.

***

Oh man… she thought to herself as she looked into his eyes. I should have been nicer to him.

***

She watched him as he examined her expired GA license.

"Hannah Louise Griffin," he read off.

Hearing her name got her attention. She smiled a big smile, similar to the Cheshire Cat from Alice in Wonderland. He already loved that smile.

"Have a good time, Ms. Griffin," he said as he looked into her eyes, handing her ID back.

She reached for it, but he held on to it a second longer before she gently pulled it from him.

"That's a beautiful name, ma'am"

He stepped to the side to let her pass and watched her go inside and locate her friends. He knew that he had to play his cards right on this one. She just might be dangerous.

The music was starting to play in the distance. Hank and the Steel Pistons were good. They played old cover songs from as far back as Lynyrd Skynyrd to newer sounds like Nickelback. There was a mixture of classic rock, country, and rockabilly, thrown in with some Celtic-style songs. Hank and his band could pack a house, and Chris had always wondered why they hadn't made it to the bigger venues. But for whatever reason, they had what they wanted at The Belle.

He took his bottle from the bouncer and turned it up again. Tonight would be a holiday for him. Time to let loose a little. He walked back to the horseshoe bar and pulled up a stool. The bartender poured him another shot from the bar's bottle. The atmosphere had somehow changed. Maybe it was the alcohol in him now. The music was reaching deep into his spirit. Hannah had his attention, but she was with her group.

"Hey, Preach!" said a loud voice from the other side of the bar.

Chris looked over to see Ben Sawyer, one of his Brothers.

"Hey, Ben, how's it?"

Ben made his way over, and they shook hands.

"You want to score?" Ben proposed as he passed an eight ball of coke to Chris. "This one's on me. Holla if you want more."

Chris looked down at the 3.5g vile of pinkish powder.

"Will do, bro! Thanks for looking out."

Everything in him was repelled by the thought of these drugs, but tonight he welcomed the high. He "needed it." At least, that's what he tried to convince himself. It would take away the pain, and maybe the ghost chasing him in his mind.

He placed the coke inside his vest and tried to find Hannah again. Just as he started to look, someone grabbed his arm and began pulling on him. He looked and found Marla. She was pulling him toward the stage.

"Brothers and Sisters!" Hank announced into the house microphone. "It's been over three long years, but I think if we make enough noise, we might get blessed with a song from an old friend to The Belle!"

The crowd began to cheer, and Marla pulled him to the stage.

"Let's hear it for the captain of the guard! One of the Original Eight Lost Boys! Come on, Preach. What do you say!" Hank yelled over the microphone.

Chris tried to decline the demand and pull away from Marla, but he decided to give in as the crowd's cheering got louder. Most of them had no clue who he was. It didn't really matter. If Hank was calling him to the stage, it had to be something worthwhile. He stepped up onto the stage, and he and the short Irishman hugged.

"Whatcha wanna play, Preach?" Hank asked as he handed him a guitar.

Chris sat down on a short stool on the stage and picked a tune on the strings. Hank leveled the mic for him.

"Y'all want to hear something that hits the soul?" Chris said, speaking out to the crowd.

He began picking, and the band started picking the tune up as he played.

"Y'all ever felt broken?" he said as he played. "How about something unbroken?"

The crowd exploded as he sang and picked the strings of the guitar.

As he sang, Marla danced in front of the stage. Her eyes were on Chris. He was fully aware of her presence, but his eyes searched the crowd for the unicorn in the smoke-filled pub.

He found her sitting with her friends. They watched him sing, and the crowd around them danced and sang along. He played to the crowd, but his eyes were locked on Hannah.

The old-timers used to tell him, "Even in the midst of a thousand sparrows, the raven will focus on one single bird. Nothing else matters."

Tonight, in the massive crowd, all he saw was Hannah.

"I'm still alive, and I'm still fighting!" he finished.

When the music ended, the pub was in full throttle. The band took over as Chris laid down his instrument. Marla immediately wrapped her arms around his neck. She kissed him, but his eyes remained open. Hannah was not even looking his way, but he couldn't think. The whiskey in his system, the rush of the crowd cheering, and now the stimulation of Marla on him. He couldn't focus. He had to at least talk to her again. Marla twirled in front of him as the crowd joined in on the music and dancing.

Two songs later, and after a few gulps from his bottle, he pulled away from Marla and made his way toward the men's restroom. He opened a stall and took another swig from the bottle. He took the coke from his cut and hit a bump from the eight ball that Ben had given him. The energy hit him like a baseball bat. He washed his hands and went back into the crowded pub. Just as he was coming around the bar, he and Hannah ran into one another.

"Hey, don't I know you?" he joked.

Hannah looked at him strangely.

"I'm Preach. Are you having a good time, Ms. Hannah?"

"Yeah, I came to see a friend. She's getting married soon."

"Funerals are always fun parties," he said, playfully joking around in his intoxicated state.

"It's not a funeral. It's a wedding," she said sharply.

"I know, sweets, but to me it's a funeral."

Hannah smiled to be polite and excused herself, vanishing into the ladies' room. Chris stood there, not really knowing what to do. Should he wait or just move on? He chose to move on.

Marla saw him and pulled him to a booth full of her friends and a few of his Brothers. He tried his best to focus on the crowd he was with, but his mind was fixed on Hannah Louise Griffin. The group made its way to the pool room, and he played a few games of eight ball. He was settling back into the mood of his environment. He was back. It actually felt good.

He finally saw her again. She was saying goodbye to her crowd and getting ready to leave. He made his way toward her.

"You need a cab?" he asked her as he got closer.

"No, I live a mile away. I'll be fine. But thank you," she said, watching him try his best to stand.

He reached into his cut and took out a card with his information on it.

"I'd like to know that you made it home safely," he slurred as he gave the card to her.

The mixture of Mexican cocaine and Irish whiskey was taking its toll on him.

"Thanks," she said as she took the card and walked away.

His eyes stayed on her until she disappeared into the rows of cars in the lot. He was captivated by her. He was confused by her, as well.

Ten minutes later, his phone buzzed.

Home, was the message.

"Home? Where is home?" he asked himself.

Another text made his cell buzz.

Hannah.

Chapter 15

Broken Roses

The sound of his cell phone was like dynamite going off in a mountain canyon in Chris's head. The more it rang, the closer to insanity he grew. He opened his eyes to find himself in a hotel room. The unfamiliar surroundings coupled with the massive headache from the hangover left him in a discombobulated state of confusion. Remnants of the excessive levels of powder and whiskey from the previous night's activities had made a mess of his morning already. He sat on the edge of the bed and reached for his phone. Though it had stopped sounding off, the buzzing vibration due to his missed texts and a multitude of missed calls was enough to drive him closer to permanently damaging the device.

He turned to look at the sleeping woman, partly covered by only a sheet, beside him, her head covered by her hands and part of one of the pillows. He pulled his hair back into an elastic band to keep it out of his eyes, then looked back at the figure beside him, shaking his head in a mixture of confusion and disappointment.

Jesus, he thought to himself.

He returned his attention back to his phone.

The text simply read, Call me ASAP.

Followed by another: Preach, don't leave that hotel without calling me first.

He dialed on his cell so he could listen to his voice messages. The calls were from a man he hadn't spoken to in more years than he could recall. Joseph Blevins, aka Lil Joe. The two men had ridden together for many years prior to Chris's leaving

Alabama. But in reality, there really was nothing he could think of that would merit such urgency.

"Preach, this is Lil Joe. Meet me at Cox's Grocery at noon."

"Preach, I wouldn't be asking if it weren't of grave importance. Please be there at noon," another of the messages said.

But it was the message with a single name spoken that got his attention. He would be at Cox's even though he knew it might not be the smartest decision.

Rule number seven, he thought to himself. Don't chase the rabbit into its hole.

Just as he stood up to pull up his jeans, the woman from the bed spoke, looking up at him.

"Don't you dare leave without telling me goodbye," she said as she tried to pull him back into the bed with her.

He looked down at her.

Oh boy… he thought to himself, feeling confused and uncomfortable when he saw it was Marla.

"Please stay with me a little longer," she said with a pouty voice.

He looked out the window, scanning the parking lot the best he could, then looked back at her.

"I'll see you later this evening," he said.

"Promise?" she begged.

"Yeah, why not," he responded as he tried to look at her, but his focus was on the parking lot. He had had six missed calls and three texts all from the same unknown number. One of those texts had warned him not to leave the hotel until he'd responded. How did anyone know where he was, and more importantly, why was Lil Joe warning him? Was there someone else out there?

"You want some coffee?" she said, sitting up on the bed.

He thought about it for a second and then responded, "Yeah, that would be good," pulling cash from his pocket. "Run across the street and get me a cowboy. Get yourself whatever you want."

She rushed to get up and put her shorts and boots on.

"Marla, don't talk to anyone until you come back," he told her.

She looked up at him and asked, "What's a cowboy?"

"Black coffee. Nothing in it," he answered, smiling.

She ran over to him and leaned in to kiss him, but he turned his face slightly. She kissed his cheek anyway, then hurried out of the room to fetch the cowboy coffee and some cigarettes.

He reached over to the nightstand, grabbed the almost-empty bottle of Apple Jack Whiskey, and put it to his lips. He took in a large gulp, finishing it off. He pulled the curtain back slightly, just enough so he could see Marla walk across the parking lot and go in the convenience store across the road. To the left of the building, a white SUV was parked, and the man inside was watching her cross in front of him. The man picked up his cell phone and started dialing. Chris put on his t-shirt and leather cut, exited the room, and walked to the office of the hotel. He knew that the people watching in the SUV would either sit back and continue watching or move in on him. He didn't know who they were yet. Law enforcement usually used black vehicles, not rented SUVs from major automobile rental companies.

Rule number fifteen, he thought. Knowing is half the battle.

He made his way out the office door and then doubled back to come in behind the SUV's driver's side door. Just as he reached the side wall of the building, looking in behind the SUV, he reached into his belt sheath. He started to draw out the knife located inside but then thought better of it. He didn't know who was watching him. Most likely, this man was one of the ones who had been watching him from the hill on Church Road. At this point, it could be someone connected with the Skulls or even someone from his Brotherhood.

He looked at the convenience store to see if he saw any signs of Marla. She was still inside. While she was just a pawn in this chess game, he wanted to be sure she was not in direct danger. He made his way to the rear of the SUV, dropping low to come in below the window. He had his entrance strategy prepared. He could see the man in the vehicle watching the office window, trying to find Chris, and looking across the road at the doors of the store. There was no doubt at this point that whoever this was, he was there watching Chris.

Chris reached through the open window, grabbing the man's head with his right hand and the man's left elbow with his own. Pulling aggressively, he slammed the man's head into the door frame and then forcefully slammed it into the steering wheel. The man's limp body slumped over in the seat. Chris opened the door quickly, pulling the man out onto the curb and then dropping to his knee so he could be at the dazed man's level.

"What are you watching me for?" he asked the man who appeared to be a Mexican gang member.

The man looked up at him in both shock and obvious fear and said, "No hablo Ingles! No comprendo!"

"Well, if you want to live, I'd suggest that you learn to hablas really fast!" Chris said as he began to draw his blade again, rage rushing through his veins.

He looked up. Marla stood between them and the street, coffee and a small bag of groceries in her hands. She kept looking at Chris and then back at the man on his back, her mouth open in a combination of fear and confusion. Chris looked back down at the man. He left the blade in its sheath once again.

"Why—" he started to ask again.

But the man was shaking his head, either not knowing how to respond or not wanting to. Either way, more pain was in his future if he didn't respond quickly.

He started speaking fervently in Spanish. Chris could only pick up a few words he knew.

Then Marla spoke up frantically and said, "Rose! He is asking you about someone named Rose."

She began speaking Spanish to the man. The man turned his attention to her and began speaking to her, looking back at Chris with every sentence.

"What is he saying!" Chris questioned.

"He says that he was sent to find you. He is looking for a rose bush," she said in a confused rush.

"Si! Si!" the man yelled.

Chris took the pressure off of the man's chest and pulled him to his feet. Blood was gushing from his nose, and there was a small cut along his hairline. Chris slammed his back into the side of the SUV, one hand on the man's right arm. Chris used his right hand to reach up and grasp the man's throat.

"Ask him what he is talking about! What rose bush?" Chris demanded of Marla.

She began frantically questioning the man, and Chris loosened his grip on the man's throat as the man started trying to explain himself to Marla.

"He says that he has been sent to help you find Rosa, or roses," she said. "Delivery… Letters. Messages!"

"Tinta roja! Tinta roja!" the man said repeatedly.

Chris turned and looked into the frightened man's eyes.

"What red ink?" he said as he released his hold on the man.

"I call for you! I call!" the man began repeating.

Chris reached into his pocket, pulling out his cell.

"Then call," he said strongly

Chapter 16

The Blind Spot

Chris had taken Marla back to the closest thing to safety that he could think of at short notice: The Belle. It wasn't because of the pub, but because of the compound surrounding it. Also, considering the fact that she was a loyal Sister of the club, he was sure, without doubt, that she would be taken care of.

He was, however, beginning to second-guess the reason he had originally set his course back to Valley Town. He wasn't sure what had him feeling uneasy, but his gut was sending out warnings loud and clear. And now, against his better judgment, he was heading out to meet Lil Joe. As if things weren't already a puzzle, everything had just grown even more complex with the unexpected introduction of Jose "El Obispo" Cruz. Both things had him uneasy. What he was fully aware of, though, was that he was heading blindly into both, with no one watching his back. He was traveling into a blind spot, once again breaking protocol by riding in solo. He knew that he was acting on emotion rather than logic, but he hadn't entered this world fearful, so there was no reason to start feeling that way now.

The meeting with Lil Joe was already set for noon. The time now was 11:20. He had forty minutes to figure out his situational options. He was constantly trying to think of anyone he knew that he could trust. After the last conversation he had had with Marcus, he found himself unsure of his alliances, not knowing if any even existed anymore. Everything was out of order. He couldn't call Marcus into this. He was not willing to risk that. His mentor and friend deserved better than to be dragged into a situation like this.

He could text Mac, but even after just considering it, he sensed resistance in his gut. There was one thing that had gotten his attention concerning Mac. His long-time road dog had mentioned the "rules" during their initial talk, which had made Chris remember what was commonly called the "Old Code." Mac had referred to rule number eight: Leave no room for excuses.

"If you can make excuses," Mac had exhorted Chris, "then your apology is not sincere. So, leave no room for excuses."

Chris pulled his bike to the side of the road. He quickly surveyed his surroundings. He had roughly thirty-five to forty minutes to get himself prepared. He was still thinking about the "Old Code," specifically rule number ten: Always be prepared. He had limited resources. Even if he needed an army, he would have to settle with what he had available: his own abilities. They would have to be sufficient at this point. But even on a bad day, he had pretty good odds.

"High ground..." he said to himself.

He looked for a spot on the ridgeline where he could set up a viewing spot so he could watch Cox's Grocery. The ridge across the road would work if he could locate a route to it that he could use his bike on. His Indian was not designed for off-road commutes. He would have to either find a logging road going up the ridge or, at the very least, a spot to park so that he could trek up to the spot where he would get a direct view of all sides of the store. One thing was for certain: He didn't enjoy having a blind spot and not having any cover.

Later, from his perch on the rocky ridgeline, he had a perfect view of all paths leading to Cox's Grocery. There were a few cars going in and out, but so far there were no motorcycles. Lil Joe would be riding a bike, not riding in a car, or what bikers call it, a cage. The only thing that seemed to be out of place was that the rear fence was blocked by a van with commercial stickers on the side.

He made a phone call and then made his way back down the ridge to his bike. He made sure that he could see in both directions that led to Cox's as he trekked down.

Eleven-fifty a.m., he thought as he looked at his watch.

He didn't like this game much, but he knew he didn't have any choice. The message had given him every reason to trust his old friend. However, something felt wrong, and he did not like this gamble.

Too late to turn back now, he thought to himself as he looked down one side of the road and saw a small group of bikes thundering toward him. Six to eight riders.

In the other direction, there was a set of black SUVs, a stretched black Crown Victoria sandwiched between them.

What are you doing, Chris? he asked himself. You have lost your mind.

He pulled out of his hiding place on the side of the road, moved around the cars blocking the way, and pulled into the gravel parking lot of the grocery store. He kicked down and watched the bikes pull into formation on the other side of the front lot, Lil Joe at the lead. The two men acknowledged one another, and Chris sat back and watched the bodyguards move to secure the occupants of the armor-plated Crown Victoria. Three bodyguards fanned out to the left, three moved to the right of the stranger exiting the vehicle, and two of the guards set up a watch position at the road's edge. The professionalism of the bodyguards was very impressive, and Chris was blown away by the display.

Lil Joe walked over and offered his hand to Chris.

"What's this about, Lil Joe?" Chris asked.

"It's gonna be okay, Brother. We have you covered," Lil Joe replied.

Chris watched as the last of the bodyguards filed into the store.

"That's not what I asked," he said without extending his own hand in return.

Lil Joe took notice and seemed to try to appear unaffected.

"We need your help, Preach. These men are here trying to solve an issue with a triune organization," Lil Joe began explaining.

Chris just looked at Lil Joe, his temper beginning to elevate, and asked, "Feds?"

"No, Preach. They aren't law enforcement of any type."

"Then who in the hell are they, Joe?"

"Well—"

"Who are they, Joe?"

"Preach, the man in the coat...well, he is a..."

Chris grabbed Lil Joe by his vest's leather collar. The seven other riders and two of the group's security immediately drew their weapons and focused them on Chris.

"Stop pissing around, Joe!" Chris said as he looked at the weapons all aiming at his head.

Lil Joe smiled.

Chris spun Lil Joe around sharply and forced his old friend to face the weapons. His right hand had unsheathed his Karambit blade, and its edge was firmly against Lil Joe's throat.

"I'm not so sure that you will find this position quite as humorous," Chris whispered. "So, I'll ask you again. Who is that man?"

"Greetings, Mr. Caldwell," said a British voice from the porch of the grocery store.

Chris looked at the suited man and sarcastically asked, "The freaking queen in town?"

"If you would kindly humor me for a few moments, I'd be most appreciative," the man said as he motioned for his body-guards to lower their weapons.

Chris looked at his options. There were very few. He released Lil Joe and shoved him to the ground, spinning his tactical blade with his index finger before re-sheathing it.

"Okay, we will try a different approach," he said to the man. "You obviously know who I am. Who are you?"

He watched Lil Joe regroup with his fellow riders, taking note of the Skull rockers.

"My name is Dr. James Collins," the man answered.

"Is that supposed to mean something to me?" Chris asked.

"Mr. Caldwell, I assure you that this will make sense shortly," Dr. Collins promised.

Chris's cell buzzed, and he took it off his belt to look at it.

This is Gabriel. My sights are clear. At your signal, the text read. He smiled.

"Mind if I smoke?" he asked as he retrieved a cigar.

He took his time biting off the tip and spitting it in the Skulls' general direction. Using a match, he lit it and slowly savored the first few draws.

"Okay then, let's take a walk," Chris said to the Brit as he exhaled the smoke. "You can bring two of your sentries. The Skulls stand down."

He looked at Lil Joe in disgust, still not fully understanding what had happened to his old friend's covenant with the Lost Boys.

"Have it your way," Dr. Collins said.

Dr. Collins walked down the stairs to Chris. The two men walked to the rear of the building. One of the massive body-guards stayed to the flank position, and the other took up point.

"Sergeant Sandra Dickerson," Dr. Collins began.

Chris stopped to look at him.

"She is in danger, my friend."

"In danger from what?" Chris asked, showing no obvious concern.

"The same men who killed your friend Matthew King."

Now Chris knew that he was fully involved, but he would not show it.

"I want to help," Dr. Collins said.

"Well, that's nice. What makes you think I do?" Chris asked as he moved the cigar away from his lips long enough to speak and release the thick smoke.

The man laughed and said, "If you didn't want to help, you wouldn't have come, now would you? What made you come, Mr. Caldwell?"

"Lil Joe mentioned a name."

"What name might that have been? Perhaps an Emma Callaway?" Dr. Collins asked.

Chris once again stopped walking and chewed down on his stogie before responding with, "What about her?"

He could feel his rage building as he spoke.

"Jason and Emma were my students, Mr. Caldwell. They were more than that. They were my friends," the doctor said as he humbly bowed his head.

"And!" Chris erupted. "They were my Family!"

"I know they were, Mr. Caldwell. They knew that they could count on you. That's why I'm trusting you."

"I want you to look directly behind me, Dr. Collins. If you trust me, then indulge me in an experiment of mine," Chris said with a nearly evil grin. "I will choose to trust you, sir, if you will trust me first."

"So be it, Mr. Caldwell. If you must make a point."

Chris took his phone out and sent a text. Seconds later, two high-caliber rounds hit just in front of both bodyguards. Seconds after that, though it seemed like minutes, the sound of the weapon echoed through the valley. The men turned in the basic direction of fire, their weapons drawn. Dr. Collins smiled but did not flinch. Chris never took his eyes off of the doctor as he watched his reaction.

"Tell your Gabriel that he can stand down. I'm fully aware that he could have sent each one of us to hell if you had so ordered."

Chris was confused and, in desperate confusion, asked, "Who are you? What kind of doctor are you again?"

"I am a friend, Mr. Caldwell. That is all that is important for you to know at this juncture," Dr. Collins said calmly and plainly. "This may help reassure you, though. Operation Jericho."

Chris's face changed drastically as he took a long look at the strange man in front of him, and then he sent out another text.

"Okay, I'm listening," he said as they and the security force began moving back to the store.

As Chris listened to Dr. Collins talk, he watched the faces of the sentries who walked beside them.

Fear... Why are they so afraid? he wondered.

"If we are in fact 'friends,' why all of this security?" he asked frankly.

"Patience, Mr. Caldwell. Be patient," the doctor said as his men opened the door to Cox's Grocery.

As he walked through the doors of the store, Chris realized that things were about to grow in intensity. Quickly.

Chapter 17

Breached Walls

Immediately, Chris was directed to a mobile metal detector. However, this was not his focus. The familiarity of the whole process was alarming. It was called "Ghost Protocol." The security team was following his program to the letter. He knew that if—and "if" was followed by a huge question mark—he was going to remove himself from this ever-growing labyrinth, now could be the last chance.

"Good afternoon, Preach," said a man walking out of the side storage area.

"Travis?" Chris responded in a mixture of amazement and confusion.

"Hey, little Brother," Travis answered as the security team moved into their respective positions.

Chris watched as the men set up their offensive stations.

"What's this?" he asked as he began preparing to defend himself.

Behind him, he could hear Lil Joe directing the men to secure the outer positions.

"Protocol," Travis responded.

Chris reached into his knife sheath, placing his fingers within reach of the Karambit.

"That won't be necessary, Mr. Caldwell," Dr. Collins said quickly as he watched Chris prepare himself for close-quarters combat.

Chris kept his hand ready so that he could quickly draw out his blade.

"Preach, we need for you to listen and not act out of emotion for once," Travis said as he leaned back on the counter to observe from a distance.

"We can talk just fine without me surrendering my weapons," Chris said as he watched the security team resume their positions.

"Stubborn as always," Travis said to himself.

"You aren't being asked to surrender your weapons, Mr. Caldwell. We just need to be sure that the room is secure," Dr. Collins said, continuing to try to calm the situation.

"Well, excuse me for my lack of trust. I have no idea who you are at all, and the man standing in front of me died twelve years ago," Chris said, still watching the men surrounding him.

"I understand, Preach. If you will relax, we can get you up to date," Travis said.

The lead guard checked his earpiece and then spoke into Dr. Collins's ear. Dr. Collins smiled and motioned for the security team to back off.

"This hasn't exactly gone as we had hoped. I suppose we should have prepared a little differently," Travis began. "But unfortunately, it is too late to go back. So, let us move forward."

Chris relaxed his posture but remained in a position of readiness.

"How long have you been gone, Preach? Two years? Three?" Travis asked.

"What's that matter?" Chris thundered defensively.

"A lot has changed around here, Preach," Travis said.

"Yeah, like you being miraculously resurrected? After we buried you in two thousand four?" Chris said sarcastically.

"Yeah, well, that's a story for a different time."

"What the hell is going on here?" Chris asked.

"Come sit down, Mr. Caldwell. We can get to the meat of this easily," Dr. Collins said.

"Who are you?" Chris asked, turning his attention back to the doctor.

"I am a friend, Mr.—" the doctor started.

"My name is Christopher. My father is Mr. Caldwell. So, call me Christopher. Only my closest Family, my club, and those I call my friends call me Preach. And for God's sake, stop with the 'Mr. Caldwell' crap," Chris interrupted.

"Okay, fair enough. I am a friend, Christopher," Dr. Collins said, complying.

"What makes you my friend? A dead man walking beside you? A former member of the Lost Boys outside? Oh wait... How about the fact that this 'security team' appears to be full of flunkies from my own Alpha Company?" Chris spoke brashly. "Every man standing within a two-hundred-yard radius from where I'm standing would be considered hostile in my eyes right about now."

"You have your rules of engagement. Which one is this one?" Dr. Collins asked.

"Rule number—"

"Twelve," Travis answered.

Chris looked at Travis with a mixture of resentment and humor.

"Which would be?" Dr. Collins asked, not really needing the answer to what he already knew.

"KEEP YOUR FRIENDS CLOSE AND YOUR ENEMIES CLOSER!" thundered every man in the room.

Dr. Collins and Chris were the only two silent.

Chris studied the older British doctor for a moment and then looked at the room full of armed Storm Guards.

"Well, that one would fit, but I was thinking more along the lines of rule number one," Chris said, smiling as he spoke.

Travis and Dr. Collins looked at one another knowingly.

"Yes, my friend, a Lost Boy should never ride solo. So, the question is, why have you taken this ride alone?" Dr. Collins asked sincerely as he brought his hands to his lips, waiting for Chris's response.

"I never ride solo," Chris said as he pressed the send button on his cell.

"Nicely played, Christopher." Dr. Collins smirked. "But your next move isn't necessary. Please call down your man on the hillside. There's no need for a dozen lives to be lost because of your refusal to listen."

"We know your protocol, Preach. We know that Gabriel is up on that hill. We are aware that his .338 is dialed in to fire at your next command. We also know that it is no longer a text from your cell that will signal it, but some slick body language that the two of you have prearranged," Travis added to the conversation.

Chris smiled and said, "Okay then. You obviously know everything about me. Let's even the score."

"Preach, I'm the one who arranged this meeting."

Chris and the other two men both turned their attention to the woman at the door.

"What the hell, Sandy?" Chris said, surprised by her entrance.

"I need your help, Preach," she said.

"Please, for the love of God, don't tell me you're the one who sent me the note," Chris said as his anger and a sense of hurt began to rise inside of him.

"No, Preach. The note is a mystery to us, as well," she said as she walked over to him. She put her hand on his cheek, rubbing the hair of his beard to calm him down. "I had no idea that you were coming home until I saw you at the convenience store the other night."

"We thought that we would never see you in Valley Town again after Mrs. Rose passed," Travis said.

"I loved your mama. She was my friend. I would never hurt you by using her memory to lure you home," she said.

Chris looked around the room. Travis and the doctor had moved over to the counter.

Sandy looked at them and said in aggravation, "You idiots almost started a war."

"Actually, it was Lil Joe that—"

"Excuses," she said as she turned her attention back to Chris. "I'm sorry, Preach. I am. Please hear me out. Matty was a friend to both of us. When he was killed, I got too close to solving the investigation. They demoted me back down to sergeant on the road again. Now my life and my kids' lives are in danger. I can't trust the department, the Lost Boys, or even members of my own family."

She looked up into the old warrior's eyes.

"They will kill her, Christopher," Dr. Collins said, adding emphasis on the word "will."

"Who is 'they'? And again, who are you?"

"The Butcher. And the Skulls," Travis answered.

"You will know who I am soon enough. Just believe me when I tell you that I am your friend," Dr. Collins said.

Chris again looked at Sandy, then at the security team.

"Where is—" he started to say.

"Ro is outside. And the answer to your next question is yes. These 'flunkies' are your men. They stand beside you, not us. They are here to protect you, not us," Sandy confirmed.

Chris looked at the men in their positions. The alpha of the guard looked at Chris with understanding and raised his right fist to his chest, slightly bowing his head in respect for his chosen captain. In reality, Chris was not their "Captain" anymore. He was their General, or more appropriately, their President. Chris raised his own fist.

"Aroo," he added.

The guards, in unison, let out a single reply: "Honor, loyalty, faithfulness." Then they added, "Our Captain, my Captain."

Chris smiled and looked at his friend.

"Rule number two, Preach," she said as she once again rubbed the fuzzy hair of his beard.

"Family needs you, doll face. I need you. The Lost Boys need you. These men standing in this room and outside would storm the gates of hell themselves if you asked them to."

Chris looked at Travis and the doctor again, then back down at Sandy.

"I'm not sure I can help anyone anymore. But if you need me, I'm standing beside you. Now, the next question is—" he started to ask.

"Operation Jericho, Preach. That's your answer," Travis offered.

"Understood," Chris replied.

"The Beast within has to be eliminated," Dr. Collins concluded.

Chris was not exactly sure about the meaning of that statement. He had, however, decided to stand by Sandy and his men regardless of the missing pieces to the new puzzle.

"The walls must fall, Christopher."

"When the walls fall, kill 'em all." Chris finished the mantra.

The security team and the four others made their way back outside at Sandy's suggestion.

"There's something I need you to see, Preach," Sandy said as she took his arm to lead him outside.

Chris stepped out the doors and onto the store's porch. The sun's rays were breaking through the cold gray clouds, bringing an element of warmth to the afternoon. His eyes strained in the brightness and found something that amazed him. The seven Skulls were all on their knees, their hands on their heads, Ro and Lil Joe standing guard around them. Gabriel was making his way across the main road, his weapon in hand.

"'...Fear not: for they that be with us are more than they that be with them,'" Chris whispered under his breath.

"Second Kings, chapter six, verse sixteen," Dr. Collins whispered in Chris's ear as he placed his hand on Chris's shoulder.

Chris looked in the man's crystal-blue eyes, then looked back at those he knew.

"Someone needs to begin explaining. Now!" he said with a hint of seriousness.

"Lil Joe didn't turn, Preach. He is your number-one ally," Sandy said, looking up at her dear friend.

Chris looked at Lil Joe's Skull cut.

"He contacted Robby. These men behind you now have been protecting me. The other men were hired last night to kill you, then to find me and finish the job," she said.

Chris once again looked at Lil Joe. Lil Joe offered a Lost Boy salute to his Captain. Chris nodded in agreement and in admission of fault.

"Aroo," they both sounded off.

"Christopher, you will understand soon if understanding is meant to be found," Dr. Collins said as he faced Chris.

"Anyone ever told you that your British 'riddles' suck?" Chris responded with a half-smile.

Chris looked at Gabriel and Sandy, then back at Ro and Lil Joe. He pulled his cell from his belt and started texting.

"I have to go, but keep me updated," he said as he pulled Sandy close to him. "I'll never walk away from you, Sandy. I'll stay as long as you need me."

"I know, Preach," she said, smiling. "Go." She looked down, seeing his text, then looked back up at his face.

Hey, this is Preach. Meet me for coffee at 16:00? Chris had texted.

Sure, why not.

Sandy noticed the real smile on his face. Chris looked at his watch. 14:00 on Thursday, January 10.

Good to go, then. See you soon. Wally's, off Ronald Reagan Blvd. He replied.

Okay.

"Okay, Preach. Engage," he said to himself, trying to hide his smile.

It had been a while since he had had the urge to smile without feeling guilty.

Chris watched the security team load up Dr. Collins and Travis. Ro and Lil Joe chatted on the far side of the lot as one of the sentries backed the delivery van into position to load up the other bikers. Two of the sentries began loading the extra bikes into a large horse trailer parked behind the fence. Ro mounted his bike, and Sandy hopped on behind him. They pulled in with the motorcade, and as a group they rode off to the east. Lil Joe put his hand to his chest and acknowledged Chris once more before walking toward the van of Skulls. Chris watched as the van pulled off, with Lil Joe and the other sentries following.

Chris hit his own ignition switch, making his iron horse roar so loud, it echoed across the valley's cold skies. He turned west, and Gabriel pulled in behind him. The two men rode off, side by side, and then they were out of sight.

Chapter 18

Winter Sunset

Chris had enough time to go shower and change his clothes before heading out to his meeting at Wally's. Changing his clothes was not as much of a chore as the shower itself. His long hair could be pulled back into a beanie, but his beard needed some attention. He had let it grow so long that he looked like a mountain man. Almost like an animal. Long and wild. He took the grooming clippers from his saddlebag and trimmed his beard down until it was neatly manicured. Nothing too short, but not out of control, either. He wore jeans and a t-shirt pulled over a thermal, simply because that was all he had clean. He grabbed his leather jacket and folded up his leather cut, neatly setting it on the little dresser in his makeshift room at the Lost Boys clubhouse. As he opened the door, he found Marla standing there, about to knock.

"Hey, you," she said. "You need anything?"

"No, I'm good, sweets, but thanks," Chris said as he grabbed his keys off the dresser.

"Think I can see you later? I get off at ten," she said.

Chris looked at his watch and then back at her and said, "Yeah, sure. I'll stop by The Belle later," brushing by her.

"Can I have a kiss or something before you leave?" she asked in a pouty voice.

He stopped and looked back at her. He leaned down and kissed her lips.

"I got to go. I'll see you later, okay?" he said, trying to smile at her.

"Okay, cool!" she said, almost leaping.

Chris headed out the side door as Marla made her way back to The Belle.

***

The weather was growing colder, and there was a light drizzle of rain. A drizzle was not anything to be concerned about on the motorcycle, but he wanted to play it safe. There were just too many variables right now for him to take unneeded risks.

"Say, Wayne, let me get the keys to one of the cages outside," Chris said as he approached the smoking area of The Belle.

"Take my Jeep. It's the black one up front," Wayne said as he tossed his keys to Chris.

"Awesome. Thanks, Brother."

Chris made his way through the bar and headed outside only to find Wayne's Jeep sitting just outside the doors. All he could do was smile and shake his head in amusement. Wayne's Jeep was like a tank. Oversized mud tires. Lift kit. Front winch. But what made the Jeep most interesting was the front hood, which had a customized paint job. It said Wayne's World in the Western Outlaw font. The words were encased in a skull and crossbones that were guarded by a black raven.

Only a Lost Boy, Chris thought with a slight laugh.

He climbed aboard the massive cage and headed to Wally's Diner in town. As he drove, he noticed things that he would normally miss while riding his bike. The comfort of the leather seats of Wayne's Jeep and the warmth of the H/C system were small luxuries he was unaccustomed to.

He could see the bareness of the trees and the cold, cloudy sky above. His mother loved this time of year. He never knew why. Probably because there was the hope of new life budding from the earth in a few months.

His thoughts of her drifted to the graveyard and then to the memory of her sitting with a Bible on the front porch. The many talks they had once had. He had once had a confidant he could share secrets with, such as his hopes and fears. She had not

104

always agreed with his choices, and she had never been afraid to express her opinions. He'd listened to her some and ignored her warnings often. Each time he had not listened, he would learn that she had been right. She never once reminded him, but he'd known she had her opinions.

He thought of the last sermons that he had ever written. She had never missed a chance to hear him preach. The last time his pen had written a sermon was for her last rites. He had been the one who had closed her eyes and sent her spirit to the heavens to be with the Messiah for eternity. This memory made his spirit search. His heart hurt. His emotions raged, and his voice rang out to the cold, cloudy sky.

"God, I doubt that you even listen to my prayers anymore. But if you could just help me figure out this damn note in my pocket and maybe let me say the right things in a few minutes, that would be great," he prayed, though it was faithless.

He watched the mist from winter rain begin to hit the windshield. Jeez, he thought.

He pulled into a spot at Wally's and headed inside.

"Fifteen fifty hours, January tenth," he said to himself as he looked at his watch.

I have ten minutes to abort this situation, he noted mentally.

As soon as he entered the diner, he was greeted by Mrs. Dolly.

"Hey, sweetheart! I'm so glad that you came in. I have something for you," she said excitedly as she grabbed him and squeezed him in a hug.

"What? Chiropractic treatments?" he joked as the woman squeezed him tighter.

Dolly went over to her purse and brought over a small brown envelope about the size of a credit card.

"What's this?" he asked as he examined the small package.

He shook the package and opened it to see the contents. He poured the contents into his rough hands. A small, folded piece of paper and two seeds fell out.

"I don't get it. What's the deal?" he asked.

"Read the note inside," she said as she watched Chris unfold came by. I haven't opened his Bible since he died, Christopher."

Chris looked up at her and then back at the note.

"Red ink," he whispered to himself.

The note said, Plant seeds, son. Watch them grow. Love, Wally.

On the package itself, at the bottom left side, there was a name written: Henry Callaway.

"I'm confused, Dolly."

She smiled and slid a picture across the tabletop. He looked down at the picture of Wally and him standing next to a motorcycle they had built together.

"The envelope was clipped to this photo. He put it in his Bible the night he died," she explained.

Chris looked at her, then at the picture, and then at the contents of the envelope. The writing was not the same as what was in his note, but the ink had his attention.

"Your mom used to mark in her Bible with markers and a red pen," she said, telling him a piece of the puzzle. "Your mom was who led Walter to Christ."

Chris looked up at her and said, "I love you, Dolly. I mean no disrespect, but I don't think God gives a rat's ass about me. So, let's skip the God talk."

He pushed the items across to her.

"That's your stuff, not mine," she said, her eyes disappointed.

"I'm meeting someone here in five minutes. We can talk about this later," he said as he reached out to touch her hand.

"You want a coffee?" she asked as she turned to walk away.

"Yes. Thank you, Dolly."

Chris looked out the windows of Wally's. The sun was beginning to drop low in the winter sky.

Sunset is coming soon, he thought to himself.

As he was watching the sun through the trees beyond the town buildings, he saw a dusty cloud from a blue Ford Focus make a trail to the parking lot. As he watched the woman gather her purse and jacket, he felt a strange tug in his spirit.

106

Thirty-one, his mind mused within him.

Thirty-one what? he asked back.

He watched her walk by the windows and come through the doors of the diner. He smiled as he saw her scanning the room, looking for him. In his mind, he could not begin to imagine what she thought of him. His rough exterior usually got him an instant negative reaction from people the club called "townies," or even worse, "civilians." He was not entirely sure which category she fell under…yet. All he knew was that her beauty was radiant. Intoxicating. Dangerous. He loved it. Like a boy chasing spiders, critters, and lizards in the backyard, he jumped at the adventure in her eyes.

She is just a distraction, he warned himself. Don't get attached.

He stood as she drew closer to his table. Once again, her smile melted him somehow.

Shit, he thought. I might be in trouble.

He reached out to take her hand, but she chose to hug him instead. He smiled.

Their conversation covered several different topics. Where they grew up. What they did for a living. How long Chris had been a Lost Boy. Nothing too terribly detailed. He only gave her half-truths.

He was content with letting her be what he often referred to as "the chase.

He had hardened his heart to emotions concerning women years ago. He had been burned too many times by "Loyal Sisters" trying to climb the ladder. "Townies" were just conquests. "Civilians" were just toys. He refused to let his heart be affected by a woman. He was a Lost Boy. Society saw him as a monster wearing leather.

As they continued to talk, he could feel his cell phone buzzing, but he did not want to look and be disrespectful. Thankfully, she excused herself to go to the restroom. He looked down at his phone. Six texts from Marla. He ignored them. Two missed calls from an unknown number. Two texts from the same number.

The first text said, Chris, can you call me? I hate to ask, but I need your help.

He responded, Sure, what's up? not knowing who was texting him.

I need you to go get Storm from school. Maybe you can spend some time with him before you leave?

Absolutely. When, where, and for how long?

He is at practice, side gym. Thanks.

Hannah returned to the table.

"I unexpectedly have to go get my son," he said to her.

"You have children?" she asked.

"Yeah, I'm a papa," he said, smiling.

As they waited to get the check, he watched her body language to see if his fatherhood was an issue. He could not read her.

They walked out to her car. The sun was fighting the chilly mist coming off the water that was falling in spots. Somehow, he could feel the sun's warmth breaking through the cold.

Thirty-one, he thought again.

"I'd like to see you again," he said.

"Yeah, sure. That would be good," she replied.

Chris hugged her and kissed her cheek, and she smiled. He tried to hide his own smile.

As she drove away, the sun was about to disappear, but he felt warm. The sunset was warming the coldness in him. Or was it this dangerous female?

This will be a complicated situation, he thought.

One thing that he was certain of was that she was neither a "townie" nor a "civilian." She was dangerously infectious.

Chapter 19

Sunflower Seeds

Chris went back inside to say his goodbyes to Dolly and pay the bill. When he came back outside, he sighed with contentment and climbed in Wayne's Jeep once again. It had been a few months since he had seen his sixteen-year-old son, Storm. He had planned on stopping by to see his kids while in Valley Town, but he'd wanted to get the busy work done so there would be no distractions.

Due to his wayward lifestyle over the last several years, he now had four kids. Each had a special place in his heart. He had not proven to be the best husband or partner to his kids' mothers. But still, Chris loved his children. He wished that he could have a bigger role in their lives, but he had destroyed so much with their moms that it was difficult. Not impossible, but difficult.

On his way to Valley High School, Chris saw the new Walmart on the right-hand side of the road up ahead.

I should stop and grab a few things for the kids while I'm here, he thought to himself.

He pulled the large Jeep into the parking lot and started to make his way down the rows, looking for a place to park the oversized tank. That was when he saw them. He turned in his seat to make sure they were who he believed they were.

"Marcus? Are you and Mrs. Ruth okay?" he asked as he pulled up beside Marcus's old Chevy pickup.

"Hey, Preach," Marcus said with a wave and a smile.

Mrs. Ruth looked up from her book and smiled.

"Yeah, son, we are okay. Just passing out some seeds," Marcus said.

Chris looked at them, confused, parked the Jeep and exited, and walked over to his old Irish friend and his new bride. They were sitting on the tailgate of the late-model truck. He studied them and the boxes of little brown envelopes. They were similar to the one that Dolly had given him earlier. Marcus had his old acoustic guitar in his lap and was picking away at the strings. Chris's eyes fell upon the seeds in the box.

"Marcus? Are you short on money? How much do you need?" Chris asked as he pulled a roll of large bills from his pocket and removed the money clip, ready to give Marcus whatever he needed.

Marcus looked at Chris, smiled, and said, "I have no need for your money, son. But thank you."

He continued to pick on the guitar.

A lady walked by and looked at Chris, then at Marcus and Mrs. Ruth.

"What seeds do you have today, Marcus?" she asked, smiling at the old man in overalls.

"Sunflower seeds, Mrs. Davis. How many would you like today?" he asked in a kind voice.

Mrs. Ruth acknowledged the woman and watched Marcus for a moment, then turned her eyes to Chris.

"Umm…maybe twenty this time? Is that okay?" she asked, looking at him and then back up at Chris awkwardly.

"Absolutely!" Marcus said as he counted out the envelopes and handed them to her.

The woman turned her purse away from Chris so he couldn't see inside, pulling out a twenty-dollar bill.

"I know that you don't want to take it, but I insist this time," she said as she pressed the paper bill into Marcus's hand.

She looked back at Chris and tried to smile, and Chris smiled at her out of politeness.

"You live around here, sir?" she asked Chris.

"No, ma'am. I moved away a few years ago," he answered.

She looked at him, and it looked like a light went off in her eyes.

"Are you the Caldwell boy?" she asked, looking into his eyes.

Marcus and Ruth watched the conversation.

"Yes, ma'am, I am," he responded.

"I was friends with your grandparents," she said, smiling.

"It's a pleasure to meet you," he offered.

"I almost didn't recognize you under your beard. But you have your mama's eyes," she said, touching his arm.

"Yes, ma'am," he said.

"Everyone loved Rosie. We still do."

Mrs. Ruth interrupted suddenly, catching Chris off guard by saying, "Christopher, would you pick me up a bottle of water while you're inside?"

She pulled a bill from the box of seeds.

"Of course, Mrs. Ruth, but I'll pay for it," he responded, and then he turned back to Mrs. Davis and said, "Mrs. Davis, it was a pleasure meeting you. Have a good evening."

He began walking away.

"Christopher?" Mrs. Davis called, stopping him.

"Yes, ma'am?" he answered.

She took one of the little brown envelopes and placed it into his palm.

"Plant some seeds this year," she said, smiling.

He looked at the envelope and started to decline, but then he looked at his old friend, who was sitting on the truck with his guitar, and humbly smiled.

"Thank you, ma'am," he said as he stuck the seed package into his jeans pocket.

He headed into the store to buy Mrs. Ruth a bottle of water and a present for Storm. As he walked toward the entrance, he could hear Marcus picking at his guitar and Mrs. Ruth singing a melody.

"'O they tell me of a home far beyond the skies, O they tell me of a home far away…'"

They sang together, and Mrs. Davis and a few new faces walked up to the old Chevy.

Chris stood in the doorway of the store for a moment, listening. He was lost in the tune and what the memory of it began to stir up in his spirit.

"'O they tell me of a home where no storm clouds rise, O they tell me of an unclouded day…'" they sang.

He could hear Marcus's deep, hoarse voice. The memory was like a freight train colliding with the darkness of night, taking it home somewhere in the distance. He turned again to go get the bottle of water.

"'O the land of an unclouded day, O they tell me of a home where no storm clouds rise, O they tell me off an unclouded day…'" Chris sang along in his mind.

When he exited the store, Marcus and Mrs. Ruth were gone. Marcus had left him a note on the windshield of Wayne's vehicle. It said, Come see me before you leave Valley Town. It was signed M. He looked at the bottle of water in his hand and tried to put the pieces together. When he drove out of the parking lot, he was still lost in thought about the current events.

Strange, he thought.

He turned onto the highway and headed to pick up Storm. He was not even sure if his son knew he was coming. When he arrived at the school, he saw a text on his phone.

Hey, Daddy, it's Storm. I got a ride home with Nattie. Don't leave without coming by to see me. Please don't be angry.

"Really?" he said out loud in a disappointed tone.

He hit the buttons on the touch screen and sent back, I love you, Son. Let's go fishing Saturday. Bring Nattie.

Distractions, he thought to himself.

He shook his head, smiled, and headed back to the FARM. The sun had dropped out of sight, but it was not completely dark. The sky boasted a cold twilight and had a reddish-purple haze. The bitter coldness of a Valley Town winter bit at his bones.

His thoughts drifted back to Hannah Louise Griffin. Somehow, for some unknown reason, the simple thought of her smile took the disappointment and the coldness from him.

He smiled under his beard.

Distractions, Preach. Don't let this get complicated, he warned himself.

His eyes scanned the horizon up ahead. He watched a large black bird as it landed on its perch in the power lines above him.

A Harbinger, he thought to himself as he drove past the raven.

Had he not known better, he would have sworn that its gaze was on him. He slowed the Jeep to look at it.

Chapter 20

Jamey Moon

The ride back to the FARM was filled with thoughts of resentment, anger, and rage and innate desires for hope, happiness, and some type of rest. Regardless of the good thoughts, Chris's mind battled in an emotional warzone, a mental and emotional game of chess. He needed a "distraction." He did not care what it was. He just needed something to mask the physical pain and emotional torment he was fighting.

There was a potentially destructive war raging inside of him. His kids lived with their mothers, and he had only seen them a few times since he went to Murphy. He had failed them. He knew it was his fault, as he could have made more time for them. He had not been able to keep his promises. His past haunted him. He had once been on the right path, but now he felt as though he had ignored anything that could have been remotely "right." He had lost a wife and several girlfriends along the way. He felt lost. Empty. Unforgivable. What had the Saunders boy called him? Forgotten. And his soul had grown cold and hardened. He held too much anger and negative feelings toward Valley Town. It was hard for him to come back. He was surprised that he was here now.

He drove down Williams Road, which was a mile away from Old Church Cemetery.

"O they tell me of a home where my friends have gone, O they tell me of a land far away, where the tree of life in eternal bloom…" he sang softly as he drove along. "…sheds its fragrance thro' the unclouded day, O the land of cloudless day…"

He turned, nearing the old church.

"…and His smile drives their sorrows all away…"

"…that no tears ever come again…"

His song stopped as he looked at the landscape ahead. This was where she was, or at least where she lay at rest. His counselor.

"Mama," he whispered.

I need you right now, he thought.

He had already been here once since he came back to Valley Town.

The moon fought to cast light in the cloudy night sky. The sudden pull on his heart to talk to someone who could give him a touch of affirmation overcame his soul. The longing pulled him to the "boneyard." He needed a drink. He needed some coke. He needed "distractions." He knew his mother would not approve, which ultimately added to the ever-growing condemnation he felt.

All the blood he had shed. All the rage and anger he had released. All the lives he had destroyed. All the lies he had told to get what he wanted. All the women who had loved him, the ones he had loved. It had been his fear of commitment and sabotaging ways that destroyed each relationship he'd been in since he was seventeen.

Excuses. Rule number eight. LEAVE NO ROOM FOR EXCUSES! he shouted in his mind. Yeah, I need distractions.

He reached into the backseat of Wayne's Jeep.

"Nothing like traveling with a friend," he joked as he pulled the almost-full bottle of Jameson from the floorboard.

He parked the Jeep and opened the bottle of whiskey. He looked at the moon's smile. It was as if it was making fun of him from the heavens. Across the large field of granite and marble gravestones, the old church sat. The cross on top of the bell tower seemed to mock him in his thoughts. He felt the anger growing. He took one drink, then two, then three. He got out of the Jeep, the bottle in hand, and approached his mother's plot. He stood and looked down at the quarter.

"Token for the ferryman."

He stood in silence. Every few minutes, he took one drink after another. Then his silence was broken. The rage. The painful thoughts. The sorrow. The loneliness. The constant condemnation. The depression. The rage. The tormenting feeling of guilt. Then the flood gates finally burst open within him.

"WHY!" he screamed at the sky. "WHY DID YOU HAVE TO TAKE HER!" His emotional torment rushed out of him. "I GAVE UP MY LIFE TO SERVE YOU!"

He shook his fist into the night sky, took another drink, and slung the bottle, now only a little more than a fifth full, at the old church.

"I NEEDED YOU! WHERE WERE YOU!" he cried. "I FOLLOWED YOUR WORD! I TRIED!"

He dropped to his knees, tears running down his reddened cheeks, his beard soaked from the mixture of Irish whiskey and tears.

"You could have taken me. Why her?" he wept. "She was good. I'm a monster. She was all I had."

The cold winter mist seeped into his clothing.

Distraction, he thought as he wiped his eyes.

He pulled his loose hair from his face and then took his phone out and sent a few texts. He sat on the cemetery's damp soil in the cold silence. The winter evening was giving him misty rain, and a crescent moon peeked through the clouds above.

He rested his hand on the headstone and whispered under his breath, "I'm sorry. I'm sorry."

He tried to stand but quickly dropped once again to a single knee. When he tried to catch himself on the gravestone marker, he knocked over the flowers and the quarter fell to the dirt. He dug in the dirt, trying to find the coin.

Over twenty ounces of whiskey consumed in a matter of minutes. His throat burned. His mind was racing as his body began to quickly react to the effects of the brown liquid.

You okay? one of the texts said.

Where are you? said another.

I can't right now, baby, said another.

Where are you? a fourth text said.

The first number: Preach?

The second number: Chris?

The third number: Baby?

The fourth number: Preach?

A fifth number: Who is this?

He drunkenly sent the same text to each of them: Es una buena noche para morir!

The responses flowed back.

Is this Preach??

Tell me where you are!

Stay where you are. Wayne will come get you.

What's going on, lil Brother? Where are you?

Chris? Where are you? Are you in Valley Town?

He put his phone in his pocket just as he began to lose his balance on his knees. He put one hand on the cold ground to stabilize himself, his intoxicated body fighting to stay up. His mind rushed backward and forward. He looked up at his mother's stone, and in the distance he could see the old church. He looked up at the clouds, which were partly covering the taunting smile of the moon. He slowly bowed his head.

"What a mess I've made. I'm sorry. I'm sorry that I couldn't save them. I'm sorry that I failed. I'm sorry that I failed to be the man I tried to be."

The whiskey was working in every part of Chris. He was getting closer to blacking out.

"I'm sorry I failed you. I'm sorry!"

He tried to stand again, but his legs would not allow it. His body crumpled beneath him, his head slamming into dirt and grass, along with the corner of the stone marker. Blood poured from his head.

His last words before passing out were, "Harbinger... Black... Han... da..."

Blackness. Silence. His body was lifeless. His face was in the damp soil. His cell phone was buzzing over and over with returned calls and texts. He was silent. Coldness surrounded him.

His lips were still trying to speak: "'In that love-ly land of un-cloud-ed...'"

From there, no words would come out in an intelligible language. There were only broken sounds. The whiskey gave him limited rest. His spirit screamed in agony. His soul longed for rest. Nothing in this life could give him what he was searching for. His "friend" Jamey had left him lying next to his mother's grave, not a single soul knowing where he was, as he grasped the ferryman's token. His last words to any of them were not even in a language they spoke.

"Es una buena noche para morir," the Spanish phrase said.

He had learned limited Spanish from working the drug and gun connections that his club had established throughout the years.

Es una...buena...noche...para...morir... Or is it morta? he thought as he drifted off into a drunken sleep.

Rule number one, Preach. What's that rule? said the voice within his mind.

Chapter 21

Brownsville

"What's on that truck, Preach?" the Kid asked.

"Don't know, don't care," was Chris's response.

"How do we know what we are protecting, then?"

Chris turned to look at the probate, his dark-brown, almost coal-black, eyes staring at the Kid beside him.

"All that you need to know is that the rig has to get to where we are taking it," he said with conviction. "Nothing more, nothing less."

"But—" the Kid started to say.

"The only butt you need to be concerned with is yours," he snapped. "You took a job! If you don't want the task, take your butt back to Valley Town."

He grabbed the man's probate leathers, pulling him almost completely off his bike with one hand. Fear showed on the young probate's face.

"We have a job. Do it," he said as he let the Kid go. "I put my faith in you. Don't make me look like a fool."

He coldly spat at the Kid.

"Everything okay, boys?" asked a voice behind them.

"Hey, Marcus, it's good to go," Chris assured his elder Lost Boy.

"Can't tell," Marcus said as he caught Chris's eye. Then he turned and barked at the Kid, "What's rule number one, probe?"

"Never ride alone. Never leave your wing," the Kid sounded off like a private in the military.

"That's right, probe! Stop asking questions and stick to your wings!" Marcus commanded.

"Yes, sir," the Kid responded, which was customary fashion.

Marcus looked at Chris, and they both looked at the red-faced, scorned, and embarrassed probate. Marcus smiled at Chris, and

Chris knew the hidden meaning behind that smile. Chris had once been sitting right where the Kid was. Marcus had sat in the same seat as Chris. They had both traveled the same path as the Kid. What they now knew, which the Kid did not yet realize, was that the "rules" were designed for one single purpose: to bring everyone home. No one would ever be left behind. The rules were set up to help teach the newest probates, and they served as a reminder to the most legendary members. Regardless of rank. Regardless of how long they had worn the club's colors. It meant something important. Something that had to be carved into the hardest of heads. Ultimately, it was what would make or break a probate. If he could not handle the task, he was not worthy of the colors.

The driver of the eighteen-wheeler cranked up its loud diesel engine. The two Suburbans pulled into their positions, one in the lead, one at the rear. Eight Lost Boys were riding in two-man formations, four in the leading SUV, four in the flanking SUV. They fell into place like a well-tuned machine.

"Let's ride!" Marcus yelled as the SUV in front of him started moving.

He raised his left hand and signaled for the wheels behind him to follow.

Twenty miles to go. The long ride had been taxing to the new riders and entertaining to the vets. The Kid rode to Chris's right side. Chris could sense the young man's nerves even from the road. He looked at the probate, moving slightly ahead to get his attention. He pretended to pat the pavement with his hand and raised a thumb, indicating that it would be okay but telling him to try and relax.

Chris knew the risk they had taken bringing the Kid on this trip. It was time to see if he was meant to be a Lost Boy or not. The team needed to know if they could count on him. If he proved himself, which Chris was confident he would, he would be a valued part of the unit. He would be part of the Family. A Lost Boy.

The trip had been uneventful so far. Chris and Marcus had been rather content with that. For the most part, these trips had always been easy. Drop off one rig. Follow the replacement rig home. Keep it simple. Do not make things complicated. This was simply a routine trip.

Over the years, the ghost unit had made its arrangements with local law enforcement to make the path straight. The Thirteens had been loyal business partners for over a decade. Their organization was controlled by Emanuel Cristos, aka "Papi." Only fools would be deceived by the innocence of a Christian-sounding name. This Catholic immigrant from Mexico was far from a saint. He was, however, famous for his methods for handling anyone who had betrayed him, lied to him, or stole from him. They vanished. End of story. The Lost Boys had a relationship of trust with "Papi."

"Nothing to worry about, Kid," he had told the young man back in Valley Town the day before.

At that time, twenty-two-year-old Charles Cleo Callaway, or "the Kid," which was what he had been referred to for the last eleven months, crossed the parking lot so he could reassure his pregnant wife that everything would be okay.

To Chris, the Kid was his friend. Charles had been a "hang around" for a few months when Chris had first recruited him. That had been over a year ago. The two had become very close. The Kid had listened to Chris's instructions and had always given him his best. Chris loved that kid, and his young wife was a beautiful and supportive companion. She was unusually faithful for a "townie." Chris loved them both like his own children. He watched as the two newlyweds spoke in the parking lot of the RV park.

"I'll be home in a few days, baby," he assured her. "I'll bring home enough money to get us a real home. We can even go get some pretty things for Anna."

He took a knee to kiss her belly.

She smiled at him and kissed his lips, saying "Well, go then. But come home before the weekend."

"I love you, Emma."

"Go before I make you stay," Emma teased.

The Kid turned away and returned to his motorcycle, which was beside Chris's.

"Charles, I love you with all my heart. This little girl loves you, too," she yelled as she smiled at her husband and rubbed her belly.

Chris looked over at the Kid as he kicked down his bike beside him.

"You good, Kid?" he asked, smiling.

"Good to go, Preach," the Kid responded.

Two by two, Marcus, Luke, Rebel, Twin, Sammy, and Eighty-Eight began falling into position. The point and post SUVs found their positions, as well. Lunch box, Devon, Miles, and Frankie were working the SUVs. The rig driver gathered his gear so he could switch cabs and prepare for the return trip. Chris watched his small band of Lost Boys, which resembled a machine, everything working perfectly and precisely, like an intricately crafted timepiece.

Across the parking lot, Papi's crew headed toward them in the second rig, followed by a group of large SUVs. Chris nudged Marcus as he noticed one of the SUVs stop short of the others. Marcus acknowledged Chris with a nod and whistled at the Lost Boy SUV drivers to get their attention. They saw the rear SUV stop and moved into secondary positions.

Chris looked over at the Kid, who was unaware of what was going on. He hit him on the shoulder with a light pat.

"Be alert, Kid," he warned. "Something isn't—"

The first bullet hit Twin in the forehead, blasting the back portion of his skull into the pavement behind him, nearly taking his head completely off his shoulders. Chris shoved the Kid off his bike, causing both himself and his friend to crash painfully on the hot parking lot concrete.

"Luke! Secure Marcus!" Chris yelled as he drew his weapon, firing at the SUVs in the distance as they opened fired on the Lost Boy positions.

The Kid followed Chris, and the two men found a safe spot behind a large concrete pillar.

"Protect that rig, Kid!" Chris yelled between rounds.

The Kid stayed right on Chris like glue.

Chris looked back at Luke and Marcus. The two warriors were working their way toward the rig as they returned fire. A second high-caliber round sounded, and it ripped Sammy's skin clean off his knee on his left leg. His battle buddy, Eighty-Eight fired his .45 caliber at the oncoming assailants. He took out three of the men who had been heading their direction. Eighty-Eight started to grab Sammy, but the third round ripped through his chest, clearing his flak jacket. Chris knew there had to be a .50 caliber hidden somewhere in the distance. Sammy was still somehow in the fight. He continued to fire at the SUVs, which were now moving to a closer position. Bodies were everywhere as the Lost Boys returned fire from their positions.

"We have got to find that sniper, Kid!" Chris yelled.

The Kid agreed, and they began moving as one body, Chris firing at the left SUV, the Kid firing at the right one.

"Marcus!" Chris yelled.

Marcus looked in his direction, and Chris gave him a hand signal that prompted Marcus and Luke to change directions and move into a secondary protocol.

"Ghost! Ghost!" Chris commanded.

Chris and the Kid made it to Sammy. The Kid grabbed the "pull" on Sammy's flak jacket, underneath his colors. Chris stepped over Eighty-Eight's lifeless body and instinctively checked for a pulse he already knew would not be there.

"Get Sammy out of the line of fire of that fifty!" Chris yelled at the Kid. "I have your six! Move! Move!"

The .50 fired off again, barely missing its mark this time. Chris turned to see a large hole now forming in the motorcycle behind him. The sniper regrouped and fired at the gas tank of the Harley Fatboy beside Chris, the Kid, and Sammy.

Chris grabbed the Kid's shoulder and commanded, "Kid! Get Sammy to safety!"

"I won't leave you, Preach!"

Chris looked at him and pulled him close, saying, "Sammy is your wing now, son. Protect your wing!"

The Kid looked at Chris, then at Sammy, who was starting to slow down.

"Charlie!" Chris said as he looked at the Kid. "I need you to protect Sammy!"

Chris scanned the lot. Behind him, Marcus and Luke had secured the rig. The driver's body lay in a heap over his travel bag, his weapon still tightly gripped in his hand. The gunmen from the SUVs had hit their mark. The driver of the Lost Boys' lead Suburban was wounded but was still returning fire. The second Suburban showed no signs of action. Chris was not sure of their situation. He then turned to look out into the distance.

"They are using ghost strategy! They know our every move!" Chris yelled to Marcus.

The sniper's weapon fired a round at the Kid and Sammy.

Amateurs, Chris thought to himself.

No real sniper would give up his position so easily. He was starting to make mistakes that Chris could capitalize on. He whistled to get Marcus's attention. Marcus read Chris's hand signal and spoke to Luke. Luke retreated to the driver's side of the rig.

"Kid! Hold your position!" Marcus yelled across at him.

Chris began his forward movement toward the large SUV to his left. He fired a few shots and then replaced the clip to his G17. The Kid was positioned to fire as trained. Marcus fired at the Suburban to his right. Chris moved out into the open and headed toward the center of the two vehicles. Just as he expected, the sniper fired a shot at him as he moved forward, hitting the pavement to Chris's immediate left. Chris moved his line of fire

124

to his right. The sniper fired again, hitting exactly where Chris had previously been. Marcus and the Kid both started shooting at the Suburban in front of Chris. It was a round that sounded like thunder echoing through the air behind him. The sniper behind the rear Suburban dropped to the ground screaming. The .50 hit the pavement beside him. Chris's steps grew faster until he was at a full sprint, and then he was standing over the sniper. He looked down at the man.

"Xavier?" he said in disbelief.

The Mexican looked up at Chris and closed his eyes.

"Coward," Chris said as he fired a single shot into the man's forehead.

He moved into position behind the two dead gunmen lying beside the front doors of the Suburban. He opened the rear door, ready to fire. The body of his old ally Papi was in the backseat, his throat cut from ear to ear. A large thirteen was carved in his face.

"What in the—" Chris began.

"You okay, lil Brother?" Marcus asked as he made his way to him.

Luke was still at the rig with an M14, ready to fire.

"Is that...?" Marcus asked in dismay.

"Yeah, and Luke hit Xavier in the throat," Chris said as he looked for the Kid.

The second rig sat idling in the distance. The driver lay on the ground, his throat cut like Papi's. The two men looked at one another, then back at the carnage of Mexican Thirteens and Lost Boys.

"Eighty-Eight, Frankie, Rebel, and Twin are lost," Marcus said.

"What about the second SUV?" Chris asked.

"No movement. I presume lost," Marcus said.

The lead SUV's driver was now leaning against its hood, clearly wounded and unable to move. His partner lay dead on the hot concrete.

"What's going on, Marcus?" Chris asked.

"Not sure, Preach."

"Is Sammy…?" Chris began.

"His leg is lost, but he is stable. We need to get him to Jessie's ranch ASAP," Marcus answered, and before Chris could ask, he said, "The Kid is with Sammy."

The men defensively made their way toward the secondary SUV. Luke held a firing position behind them as cover. Chris took the driver's side. Marcus took the passenger side.

"What the hell, Marcus!" Chris proclaimed, rising up and seeing Marcus have the same reaction.

"Where is Devon?" Marcus asked.

"Not on this side. Lunchbox is lost," Chris whispered as he looked down at his fallen Brother's limp body, which was lying in a pool of blood. "His throat…" he tried to say.

"It's time to move!" Marcus said as they both looked at the Lost Boy rig, where Sammy, the Kid, and Luke were positioned.

As they began to move, they watched in horror as Luke turned to his rear and began firing his weapon before falling to the ground. They spread out in a wedge to get to the rig. The sound of a 9mm could be heard from somewhere behind the rig. Marcus took one side, Chris the other. Luke was sitting against the front wheel of the cab, his face pale white. He sat staring at Sammy and the Kid.

The Kid lay over Sammy's body, his right hand still clenching his weapon, his left holding his throat. Blood was pouring out like a faucet. Chris ran to the Kid's side, pushing him to the ground. The young man's eyes were staring wildly into the distance.

"Hold on, Kid!" Chris tried to say as calmly as possible.

The Kid was trying his best to speak. "Gho…" He looked at Chris. "Van… Anna…"

He slowly faded out.

"Don't talk, Kid," Chris said as he applied pressure to the Kid's wounds. "You're gonna be okay."

126

Chris looked at Marcus and Luke and said, "We have to get them to Jessie's," his voice audibly breaking.

"Please, God," Chris pleaded. "I have to get them home. Please."

***

Chris could hear the voice of a woman and could feel a tug on his elbow as he was being awakened from the dream. It was not a dream, really. It was a vivid memory from the past. A nightmare of reality.

"Wake up, baby." Marla's voice broke through the dream. "It's okay, Preach. It's just a dream."

He rose up from the bed. Confused. Disoriented. His eyes tried to focus. He looked at Marla, then around the strange room.

"Where am I?" he asked.

"You're at my apartment. Do you not remember coming here last night?" she asked.

"How? Why?" he asked, attempting to stay calm.

"You got wasted last night. We had to track you with Wayne's Jeep's GPS," she said as she continued trying to console him.

Chris sat up in the bed. He looked down at his naked body.

"Did...?" he started to ask.

She laughed and answered, "Yes, baby, we did...again."

He looked at her body.

"Oh boy," he whispered.

"You think it might be possible to be together and you actually remember?" she asked, visibly upset at the situation.

Distractions, he thought. Jesus, Preach, what are you doing?

"What a mess this is becoming. I have got to get out of Valley Town!" he said, disturbed by the current situation.

Marla was not the problem. He knew that he was the problem. She just wanted to be loved. He just wanted distractions.

His agitation grew once he stood up and walked over to the little corner table. There, he looked down at the remains of an eight ball of cocaine.

What are you doing? he thought.

Marla stepped out of the bathroom and was wearing his long-sleeve shirt, which she must have found in his saddlebag.

"I washed your gear," she said as she came up behind him, wrapping her arms around his waist. "I'll be a good girl for you, Preach." She looked up at him. "I'll do anything you ask."

He looked down at her and said, "I'm leaving in a few days, Marla. This isn't gonna work out the way you want."

"I'll be yours while you're here, then," she offered.

She was hoping he would change his mind.

His thoughts went back to the Kid. The chaos at Brownsville.

Was that twenty years ago? he asked himself.

"What, baby?" Marla asked, trying to help.

He looked at her again and said, "Nothing, sweets," trying to smile at her.

I am so sorry, Kid, he thought to himself.

He stood looking in the mirror in Marla's bathroom. His mind drifted back to the memory of the dreadful day in Brownsville, Texas.

***

"Luke, what happened?" Chris asked his Lost Boy Brother, who was sitting in a chair in Jessie Turner's kitchen.

"He came out of nowhere, Preach," Luke began explaining. "I heard the Kid call out..." He tried to continue but got lost in emotion.

Chris and Marcus waited patiently for Luke to recover his thoughts.

Luke looked up at his two Brothers and said, "That Kid saved our lives. He fought to protect Sammy and me." He lost it there and was unable to finish.

"Jessie and Patty are in there with the Kid," Marcus said as he put his hand on Luke's shoulder. "Sammy is stable. His leg is destroyed."

Chris looked up at Marcus and asked, "The Kid?"

"I don't know, Preach," Marcus said again. "Luke said that it was a single man with no firearm. Just a blade." He began to try to piece the story together. "The Kid fought him off and protected his wing. He never left Sammy."

Chris just stared off into the distance.

"Devon," he said under his breath.

Marcus saw the rage building inside of Chris and started to say, "We don't—"

"Yeah, I do. I know it was Devon," Chris said angrily.

Jessie came out covered in blood. Chris already knew what news was coming. His rage grew rapidly.

I will find him, he thought to himself.

Jessie handed him an envelope covered in blood. It had to have been taken from the Kid's hand. The envelope had only one name written on it: Preach. Chris looked up at Jessie and the others.

"I'm sorry, Preach. I tried, but he lost too much blood," Jessie said, trying to console his friend.

"No. I have to get him back home to Emma," Chris said, not accepting the news.

"Preach…" Marcus began. "The Kid died protecting Sammy. He saved Luke's life, and the truck is still secure."

"No! Dammit! He has a baby coming! I have to get him home," Chris said, staring off into the dark room where his young friend's lifeless body lay.

The cold, stainless-steel table had been designed to treat animals. Not boys. Not friends. Not Family.

***

Once again, Marla brought Chris out of his daydream.

"Preach! Preach! Baby, are you okay?" she asked with genuine concern.

Chris's emotions were overwhelming him, but he tried his best to hide them from Marla.

"Yeah, I'm good," he said, trying to respond and think at the same time. He looked at her, then at his saddlebag. "Do you have my cut?"

"Yes, baby. I have all of your stuff."

He thought about the whole situation again and said, "Marla, we can have a good time together. I don't want to play games with you."

She looked at him in surprise and appeared to be hurt by the rejection.

"You're an awesome chick," he added.

"But—" she tried to interject.

"Stop, Marla. I like you. But I'm leaving in three days," he snapped. "I can only give you that."

He started looking around the bedroom. He grabbed his clothes and put them on, then gathered his gear and left her standing in his shirt, alone in her bedroom. He headed for the door. As he had guessed, his motorcycle was parked in the spot just outside her apartment, where Wayne had left it.

Chapter 22

Blood Money

"Señor Jorge promised that he would have the money tonight, Señor," the timid little Mexican told the man looking out the window of the room in the high-rise office building.

"Excuses, Raphael. You know that I don't like excuses," responded the man who was sharply dressed in a black, tailored Christian Dior suit.

Raphael looked around the room, his fear quickly growing more intense as his eyes bounced from the suited man facing away from him to the man sitting in the shadows.

"Señor, please forgive me. I have told you everything that I know," Raphael said rapidly, his voice shaking.

"Oh, my dear friend. I am not concerned about the money," the suited man said with a slight grin. "Money is easy. I want respect."

He clenched his fist in the air.

Raphael looked over at the man in the shadows of the room. The morning sun was hitting his face just enough to blind him, blocking his view.

"Señor, I do respect you. You know that?" Raphael whimpered.

"It's not your respect I demand, idiot."

The suited man lit a Cuban cigar and waved his hand in the air. The stranger in the shadows rose up from his chair and walked over to Raphael's left side, reaching down and grabbing the smaller man just under his armpit, standing him up. Raphael looked up at the stranger. The man's long black hair covered most of his face. The only thing really recognizable about him were the scars and the remains of once-burnt flesh.

"Send a message. But leave him alive," the suited man commanded his henchman.

"Absolutely. I'll send a message," the man assured him.

"Please! Señor Cruz, please!" Raphael begged.

Cruz looked at Raphael and then at the stranger and ordered, "Make it painful. I hate to hear a man beg. Pathetic idiot."

He turned back toward the view from his office, and the man shoved Raphael toward the door.

"Let's not forget my part of this contract, old man," the henchman said, looking back at Cruz.

"Primo, you will get what you desire," Cruz said as he blew out smoke from his expensive cigar. "Oh, and bring me a trophy."

"Absolutely," the stranger promised.

The stranger forcefully led Raphael to the door, only stopping long enough to pick up a backpack with stacks of unmarked American currency and two kilos of cocaine. He opened the door, and the two stepped into the lobby.

"Call the contact at the department. Tell them where to find the bodies," the stranger said as he handed Raphael and the bag to the two men waiting just outside the office. "I have the perfect message to leave."

Two hours later, the remains of two unidentifiable bodies would be found floating down DeSoto Falls. The message: Anarchy breeds chaos.

Chapter 23

Harbinger

The biting cold mountain air chilled Chris to his bones. The morning ride was beautiful. While riding along the curvy road that had been cut through the pines of Cloudland Mountain years ago by the armies of the Union, he thought of the events that had occurred since his return to Valley Town. The Lost Boys seemed to have lost their original purpose: Family. What had once been built to be a unification of Brothers watching over one another was now unrecognizable. No longer helping when help was needed. No longer standing up and preparing to protect the club and the Family with their lives.

I am my Brother's keeper, he thought to himself.

They had made a pact to always be there for one another. Through whatever came their way, they would stand together. He had seen the evidence of that belief in the Brothers who came to Church. Those in the courtyard. Those in the clubhouse. But the leadership had changed hands since he had left Valley Town. The purpose had changed. The only thing that seemed to matter now was the hunger for power. Drugs, guns, and women had always been staples of the "Family" way, but now that had somehow evolved into an apocalyptic mess. The "Loyal Sisters" were no longer respected parts of the community. They were less than animals. Their bodies were no longer their own. They were used, sold, and traded off so their owners could get money. Now the Loyal Sisters fought to live. They vied for their own places of power.

Marla, he thought.

She was just a kid, really. She was twenty-three years old. The club had taken her from the streets and gotten her away from a

ho had used her to "entertain" his comrades. When
her, she was so drugged up and dirty that it was
o tell her age. Her physical state made it difficult for
some to be sure if she was even human anymore.

That was what the club was about: protecting the weak.

I am my Sister's protector, he thought.

Now it seemed that the "code" had been forgotten.

Maybe that's the truth in the Saunders boy's words. The original purpose of the club was forgotten.

He clenched his muscles, thinking about how what had started with eight men had grown into thousands of individual families that ultimately formed one Family. But somehow, the Family had failed. Was it the club that failed? Was it the original code that failed? The leadership? The vision? It was all broken now. What was it that Rockhound had said as he walked back to his bike?

We needed you.

Rockhound's words echoed in Chris's mind.

You disappeared. Do it again!

The words rattled Chris's mind. He could feel his rage building up.

How was it my fault? he asked himself.

He could hear a voice taunting him inside his head, creating havoc within his soul. It was ripping him apart. It was breaking him down.

You left your men behind. The Loyal Sisters were left unprotected. You broke the code. You failed. Why did you come back, Preacher Man?

That last question rocked him.

I'm not a preacher. I'm a monster. I failed, he thought. Anybody can stand up and say pretty words that give an emotional experience to the butts sitting in those seats.

His thoughts raced.

You are NOTHING! the voice inside his head screamed.

He could almost hear the laughter of the one speaking to him in his thoughts. But how could that be possible? He was not laughing. How could he hear himself laughing?

You came back to Valley Town for a purpose, Preach, he thought once again.

Yeah, to die. This is where it should all end, Preacher Man, the taunting voice replied. Go buy a bottle of whiskey and pop some more pills. End this mess, Preacher Man!

"Marcus," he said to himself as he saw the image of his old friend in a memory.

Go see Marcus. The thought was a calming salve.

No. Marcus will just make things harder. Go get the whiskey, the voice teased.

Up ahead were the crossroads. As he stopped his bike, he looked up into the morning sky.

The sun was starting to warm things up a few degrees.

"God, I need your help," he said out loud. "I know that I'm not deserving of anything, Lord, but I can't—"

Just as he murmured the last words, up in the tree line, he saw the large black wings of the raven as it flew.

"Harbinger," he whispered.

Go see Marcus, the calming voice said again.

He watched the bird fly from its perch and go in the direction of Marcus's homestead. He turned his bike and followed the Harbinger. It was almost as if the bird of prey was leading the way. He followed.

One of the voices screamed in his mind, You're wasting time! Turn around!

Please, Chris thought as the war inside him raged on.

Follow me, Preach. Trust, the more calming of the voices said.

He followed the Harbinger.

Chapter 24

Running Wild

Chris made his way down the mountain road, fighting the voices within. The raven had disappeared somewhere in the treetops. He turned onto Roper Church Road. He had taken this route many times and knew that he could navigate it blindfolded.

Mrs. Ruth was sitting and reading near a window of her house when he arrived and kicked down his bike. He watched her for a moment while removing his gloves and riding gear. He was still puzzled about how she and Marcus had married.

Logic must not be popular around this town anymore, he thought to himself.

His mind battled for the main position with the multitude of ghosts chasing him.

"Hey, lil Brother," Marcus said as he stepped out of the garage.

Chris looked up at his friend and smiled. He took one more glance up at the house. Mrs. Ruth was now standing in the doorway, waving down at him. He returned his attention to Marcus after returning her greeting.

"What are you doing out so early?" Marcus asked.

"Umm," Chris began. "Well, to tell you the truth, I had a hell of a night last night. I woke up this morning with a hangover… and Marla lying beside me."

"Again?" Marcus jokingly asked him.

He wiped the oil off his hands and looked up at the house.

"Hope you want some coffee and biscuits."

Marcus grinned, and they looked up to see Mrs. Ruth making her way toward them with a tray of coffee and biscuits.

"Christopher, I didn't know if you wanted honey or jam, so I brought both," she said, smiling.

"Thank you, ma'am," he said as he took the mug of black coffee and a biscuit.

"You want creamer, milk, or some sugar?" she asked.

"Cowboy is fine, ma'am," he said, smiling back at her.

"Boys," she joked back.

Chris watched as Mrs. Ruth walked to her husband, taking his hand and looking at his fingers.

"Those had better be washed before you eat," she said in a motherly tone.

She kissed him and walked back to the house, and Chris watched Marcus's eyes follow her up the steps and out of sight. The retired Spanish schoolteacher resumed her spot in the window with a book.

"Come up here and see what I'm working on," Marcus said, motioning toward the garage with his mug.

The two men walked into the heat of the garage. The late-model Harley Davison sat in the rack.

"This old panhead has me busy," Marcus said. "It's a good distraction."

Chris looked at the workmanship on the custom leather seats sitting on the table beside the rack.

"These are nice, Marcus," he said with true enthusiasm.

"My lady did the work. I'm thinking about burning a design into them," he said with the pride of an artist.

"Cool," Chris offered, not really knowing what to say.

Chris felt Marcus watching him as he made his way around the garage, looking at the old panhead on the rack. They both sipped their coffee in silence as he walked over to a little desk. He picked up a picture frame and looked at the image for a second.

"Those were good days, lil Brother," Marcus said, breaking the silence.

"Yeah, they were," Chris offered. "What happened around here, Marcus?"

He laid the picture of him, Marcus, Rockhound, Devon, Walter, Jessie, and Luke back on the desk. He could not help but notice the fingerprint-stained Bible that was opened up.

"A little light reading?" he playfully asked, turning the old Bible toward him on the desk. "John, chapter twelve," he read out loud.

Marcus began tinkering on the old bike and, without looking away, said, "Yeah, John is my favorite Gospel."

"Yeah, I guess so," Chris said, trying not to show any disrespect to his mentor.

Chris walked over to the multitude of pictures scattered on the wall. Trophies from drag racing events sat on the bookcases, along with owner's manuals for motorcycles of decades past and a mixture of reading materials. Harley manuals. Indian manuals. Manuals from the 1940s to the 2000s. Iron Horse magazines. Easy Rider magazines. Charles Stanley titles. Ken Hagan titles. John Eldridge titles. He looked around the room as Marcus remained silent, his hands busily working on the racked panhead.

"What's up with the seeds, Marcus?" Chris asked as he opened a box full of packaged seeds ranging from tomato to sunflower to cucumber to a variety of pepper seeds.

Beside the box were a number of bank pouches that held stacks of currency, both paper and rolled coins. That was when he saw her name next to a list of others.

"Rose Anne Caldwell. What the hell is this?" he asked as he turned around to face Marcus, who was now standing on Chris's side of the rack.

Marcus sipped his coffee before answering.

"Your mama started this thing," he said.

Chris was visibly shaken as he asked, "Started what, exactly?" picking up a seed package.

"Well, the idea, really," Marcus said, then started to explain. "As you know, your mama started working as a volunteer at the hospital before she got sick again."

Chris leaned against the desk, looking at him and then back down at the seeds. He reached into his pocket and pulled out the envelope that Mrs. Davis had given him, taking a long look at it and then looking back up at Marcus.

"That's when she met Maggie, remember?" Marcus asked.

Chris looked back up to the house, to where Mrs. Ruth still sat, and said, "Mrs. Ruth's daughter?"

"Yes, Maggie was Ruth's daughter," Marcus confirmed.

The wheels started spinning in Chris's head.

"That's when Mama started going back to that little church on Roper," Chris said out loud as he thought it out.

"That's right," Marcus said as he walked over to Chris. "When Maggie died, Ruth was a mess." He gazed at his wife in the house. "Your mama started going by Ruth's house after that. They started doing a women's Bible study. Rose Anne, Ruth, Dorothy Davis, and a few others from the church."

"What's that got to do with a box full of seeds and my mama?" Chris snapped at his friend.

"Your mama had a dream. She wanted to reach this town somehow. So those stubborn women started formulating ideas," Marcus explained.

He reached into the box for an envelope and laid it next to the one Chris had pulled from his pocket. On both envelopes, there was a Scripture. Each envelope had a different Scripture. One had Psalm 46:10 written on it. The other had Jeremiah 29:10-14 carefully written on it.

Chris thought about it for a second and remembered the little brown envelope that Dolly had given him. He reached into the inside pocket of his cut and took it out.

"Romans, chapter eight, verse twenty-eight," he read out loud.

"Where did that one come from?" Marcus asked.

"Walter had it in his Bible. Dolly gave it to me yesterday," Chris answered. "Dolly said something about Mama giving it to Walter."

Marcus started to say something but seemed to think better of it, instead grabbing his jacket and saying, "Let's go for a walk, son."

The two old friends walked out of the garage and started walking along a path leading behind the house. They stopped at the fence that separated the backyard, a small area that was last year's garden, and the pasture. In the distance, a stag and a mare playfully danced in the day's sunshine.

"The stag has to be broken this summer," Marcus said as he watched the scene in front of them.

Chris was still in deep thought about the seeds.

"Marcus? What does any of this have to do with my mom?" he finally asked.

"Love," Marcus replied.

"I don't get it," Chris said as he looked up at Marcus and then out at the horses in the pasture.

"Your mama loved this town," Marcus said. "She wanted to make a difference. Your mama brought a hint of love back into the heart of Valley Town. She started a movement. She didn't know what she had started, but her love created a reaction of love that moved through the lives in Valley Town."

Chris sipped his coffee and continued to watch the horses. Visions of his mom's smile rushed through his mind.

"Your mama introduced me to Ruth," Marcus said.

The stag made a loud noise, catching the men's attention.

"I was lost, but because your mama loved you, she loved me," Marcus said as he put his hand on Chris's shoulder. "I was broken as a man. I was tired. The way the club was moving, I felt like I was being pulled into a black hole. I was like that stag. I needed to be broken. I needed something to break me. Ruth came into my life. I was just like everyone else in that club. I was lost."

Chris leaned against the fence and looked through the sliding glass doors leading into the little dining room beside the kitchen. Mrs. Ruth had her book in her lap. Her head was lowered. He thought it was odd that she could fall asleep in such a strange position.

"Your mama planted a seed, son," Marcus said, pulling an envelope from his jacket and pouring out the seeds in his hand, the tiny black and white seeds mixing with the hardness of his dirty, aging, callused Irish hands. "Rose Anne planted love into my life. I never thought I could love a woman. I mean, really love one. I only knew how to use them."

Chris watched as his mentor and friend smiled while watching his wife through the glass doors.

"I never knew love could be this real." He smiled. "Your mom sowed a seed in Ruth. She sowed a seed in me. She never got to see those seeds harvest, but I believe she knew."

He looked at Chris and asked, "Do you have the note that you found in Murphy?"

Chris reached into his wallet and pulled out the crumpled light-brown paper. He unfolded it, and the writing fit almost perfectly with the envelope in his hand. He handed it to Marcus.

"I can't explain the red ink," Marcus said. "But it is your mama's writing. And it's written on one of these seed packets. But from what I know, that's not possible.".

"Why?" Chris asked.

"Because we didn't start passing the seeds out until the spring of two thousand fourteen,"Marcus said, looking back into the house.

Marcus looked in the horses' direction and then back to the seeds in his hands.

"Thank you, Father," he whispered under his breath.

Chris was in his own thoughts and thought little of what Marcus said.

"Do you know what chapter twelve of John talks about, Preach?" Marcus asked.

"No, not really. I can't tell you the last time I picked up the Bible," he confessed to Marcus.

"I've learned throughout my years of running from God, and even more so since He broke me like a wild stallion, that the best lessons often come from seasons of pain. I didn't realize it for a long time, but after the Kid was killed, I began burying myself deeper and deeper into a miserable state of chaos."

Chris immediately looked at Marcus. How could he have known about the dream? The nightmare? The horrible memory of that day down in Brownsville?

"God has an uncanny way of working His love into the darkest soil," Marcus continued. "He uses the soil to reshape us and make us move back toward His divine purposes. That day in Brownsville almost sent me to a place of insanity. I watched my best friend fade away right in front of me." He looked at Chris. "You began drifting away at that point. After your mama died, I wasn't surprised that you took off. I half expected you to. I failed you because I hadn't learned how to help you yet."

Chris could only look at Marcus as he listened to him talk.

"Ruth helped me heal. After you left, my world collapsed in front of me. Your mama's love for you brought Ruth's love into my life. True love never fails," Marcus said, looking down at the seeds and then back at Ruth inside. "Your mother's love for 'her Valley Town' was put into seeds that were sown into the hearts and lives of everyone she knew. Many reaped a harvest from heaven because of her vision"

He reached into his jacket pocket and removed a small New Testament Bible, flipping it open to John 12. Chris fought the urge to roll his eyes. The last thing that he wanted was more useless religion. But out of respect for Marcus, he continued to listen.

You're an idiot, the voice said. The whiskey would have been better than this meaningless conversation. You could have spent the day in bed with Marla. You need a distraction!

Marcus's voice finally overthrew the one in Chris's head.

"Jesus gave us a wonderful visual of what it means to be broken. He compared the lives of believers to a single grain of wheat." He opened up his hand again, displaying the seeds. "If you hold a seed in your hand, nothing will happen. If you put it into a little envelope to keep safe, it will stay there until you open that little envelope again. Unless you plant that seed, it's worthless."

Chris listened to his old friend speak.

"Your mama knew that you had to plant seeds to see results. In Valley Town, she planted her love," Marcus said. "It is when the seed has been placed in soil, where its protection is stripped away, that amazing things happen. Those seeds turn into something new. Your mama sowed love." He looked at Mrs. Ruth once again. "Because of her faith, she sowed her love. Ruth and I were blessed by that seed sown. We are examples of the harvest that God had promised to Rosie."

Chris fought the tears trying to leak from his eyes.

"Jesus didn't just talk a good game, Chris. He lived a life of example for us to follow. He was broken and sown into the soil of our spirits. From that brokenness came life. His single seed of love brought the harvest of countless believers. His love caused true love to break through the darkness."

Chris watched as Marcus cracked open the seeds in his hands and tossed them toward the pasture's fence line.

"Your mama brought Ruth into my life. Ruth showed me what real love is. I accepted Christ as my Savior as those women prayed over my lost soul." Marcus said, emotion in his voice. "Had your mama not sown seeds, I would still be lost."

Chris looked down at his watch.

Marcus seemed to know that he had said enough for today and said with a smile, "Let's go inside."

"I need to go soon," Chris said awkwardly.

"I know, but you have to say goodbye to Ruth."

Chris agreed. The two made their way inside the warmth of the house. Mrs. Ruth had gotten up and started another pot of coffee.

"Drink one more before you ride off, Christopher," she said, smiling.

He offered her his mug, and she poured him half a cup.

"You been by to see your daddy yet?" she asked.

"I will today, ma'am," he promised as he quickly swallowed the last drop of coffee, trying to leave before she popped him in the head.

He looked at the crumpled brown paper and the envelope of seeds in his hand.

"Make sure you read chapter twelve of John when you can, lil Brother," Marcus said as they embraced.

Chris placed the seeds and note inside his cut, walked outside, and cranked up his motorcycle. The sound of its engine roared through the pines. The three of them said their goodbyes, and the couple watched as he rode down the driveway.

***

Marcus looked down at Mrs. Ruth, took her face in his hands, and said, "What have you been doing, my pretty Spanish dove?"

He warmly kissed her smiling face.

"Praying," she said with a loving smile.

"Of course you were," he said, laughing.

She hit him playfully in the chest.

"I could feel your prayers, baby."

He looked out at the driveway and into the trees. The old raven sat perched up high above the road.

"God heard you and spoke to me," he said, kissing her again.

"I love you, Marcus," she said, beaming like a schoolgirl.

"I love you more," he joked.

"Never!" she exclaimed, laughing.

They walked back inside. After washing his hands and face, Marcus joined her on the couch next to the fireplace.

Chapter 25

Cruel Intentions

Chris rode down the highway, watching the trees and farmland slowly turn into small country buildings. His head was throbbing from the night before. He had drunk almost a full thirty ounces of Wayne's whiskey stash and had used the remainder of the "Pink Lady" cocaine on Marla's table. He was dehydrated, and his body was screaming for fluids and "goody powder." This small side of town had one little gas station. He knew it would be wise to stop now so he could get some relief from the headache ripping through his skull.

The weather was nice for a winter day. The sun was shining bright, and it gave the day enough warmth that he could enjoy the ride instead of being frozen underneath his leathers. He watched the variety of cages drive by as he pumped gas into his motorcycle.

So many things had changed in this town since he had left. Maybe it was not the town that had changed, though. Maybe it was him. The club did not seem the same anymore. Maybe he had been gone for so long that the darkness that had once loomed over the Lost Boys had escaped his mind. The drugs. The sex trade. The backstabbing. He knew it had all existed before, but it seemed much darker now.

Marcus had most definitely changed. His oldest friend and mentor was not the same anymore. He had married the church lady. Chris laughed as he thought about that description of Mrs. Ruth.

His mother had grown close to the retired Spanish teacher. Mrs. Ruth had lost her husband in a car accident back in 2010. Her daughter, Maggie, had passed in 2012. Maggie had been in the same treatment area as Chris's mom. The three women had grown close. When Maggie died, Mrs. Ruth was devastated. Mrs. Rose, his mom, began going over to her house and sitting with her, learning how to crochet. The two women became like sisters. Apparently, that's when Mrs. Rose felt God's pull on her heart to introduce Ruth to Marcus.

The thought of Marcus and Mrs. Ruth was insane. Marcus was an atheist. He had poked fun at Chris over the years for his underlying hint of Christian faith. It had been hard being a Christian and a Lost Boy, or a LoBo, as the locals called them. The two were like night and day.

Chris sat on the saddle of his iron horse, deep in thought, after the pump had stopped. His thoughts were running uncontrollably. His mind was using mental cruise control.

Mrs. Ruth had made Chris promise to go see his dad while he was home. Although he had promised, he was still resisting actually going. He was unsure if he could see his dad. The pain he felt from the loss of his mother still ripped through his soul. His father had moved on. He had fallen in love with a lady who worked at the corner market. That was one reason why Chris had left Valley Town. He had taken all that was his and vanished. He'd left both of his families behind.

Why are you back, Preach? the voice asked within him. What is 'home'?

He watched as a van pulled up to the pump in front of him. The man driving smiled at him. After the driver finished talking to the woman in the passenger's seat, he kissed her. Then the doors on both sides of the van opened, and the sounds of laughter and teasing kids filled the air.

"Be careful, boys!" the driver said as the boys chased one another. He turned to Chris. "It's a beautiful day, isn't it?"

Chris was taken by surprise but said, "Oh…yeah. Sorry, I was daydreaming."

The man smiled as he began pumping gas into his van.

"I can only imagine. It's a beautiful day for a ride," he said. "Your bike is awesome. What is it? A Harley?"

Chris looked at this man who was wearing trousers and a Polo shirt.

"It's an Indian," he answered politely.

"It's beautiful," the man said, smiling.

"Thanks." Chris tried to think of a way to be polite to this family man. "You ride?"

The man looked at his wife and kids and let out a small laugh, then jokingly said, "No. I never had the chance."

The man turned to see where his boys were running around and playing. His wife had her book in hand, laughing as the boys chased and teased one another. She patiently waited on her husband to finish pumping gas so they could go inside for refreshments.

"You from around here?" the man asked Chris.

Chris looked down at his colors and then back at the man and his family. He started to say something sarcastic but decided against it, instead saying, "Yes, sir. I grew up here. But I've been gone for a couple of years."

"Well, it was nice talking to you," the man said as he replaced the pump.

"You, too," Chris responded.

The petite woman looked at Chris and offered a sweet smile. He returned the smile and said hello to her. The man gathered his kids up into a small group, and they walked to the store. Chris watched for a second and then put up his pump so he could leave. He looked down at the area near the driver's side door of the van and saw the man's wallet lying just under the wheel. He walked over and picked it up. Without looking in the wallet, he walked to the doors to return it to the man.

You are a monster, Preach. That is what they see when they look at you, the voice told him. I bet he will look inside the wallet to see if anything is missing. Just keep it and drive off. It is his fault for dropping it.

He opened the doors to the store and looked around. The man was at the coolers holding juice and milk. Chris grinned at the family and walked over to the man, holding out the leather wallet.

I bet he will look inside, the voice taunted.

The wife looked up first and saw Chris standing beside them. She nudged her husband's arm.

"Dean," she whispered.

The man looked at his wife and then followed her eyes to Chris. He looked at Chris, then at the wallet.

"Oh man," he said. "I need to tie a rope to that thing. I drop it all the time."

Chris watched the man as he took it from his hand. He waited for the man to look in his wallet like the voice suspected he would. The voice was wrong. The man put it in his back pocket.

"Thank you, sir," the woman said to Chris.

"Yes, thank you, my friend," the man said as he reached out to shake Chris's hand.

Chris looked at the smiling woman and then at her husband. He stuck out his own hand and shook the man's soft, non-calloused hand. The contrast between the stranger's soft hand and Chris's rough, bear-like paw was like night and day. This reminded Chris of his earlier thoughts.

"No problem," he said and turned to walk away.

He stopped at the coffee counter and began to pour himself a large cowboy.

"Excuse me," the man said.

Here it comes, the voice said inside of Chris's head.

Chris looked at the man.

"My name is Dean. My friends call me DC. I'd like to buy you that coffee if you would let me," he said. "This is my wife, Rebecca, and our soccer team."

Chris looked between him and the loving mother behind him as she played with her kids. The voice inside of his head was trying to taunt, but the sincerity in Dean's tone stopped it.

"I insist, sir. You didn't have to return my wallet," he said, smiling.

"How do you know I didn't take money out of it?" Chris asked.

"It's just money. It doesn't belong to me anyway," Dean said, grinning.

"You didn't even look inside to see if anything was gone," Chris said.

The man looked at the wallet and said, "Why would I? Like I said, it's just money."

Chris looked at the kids and Dean's wife.

"I'm Preach," he said. "You have enough to pay for. I'll get my coffee. But thanks."

A look of hurt came over Dean's face.

Chris almost turned to walk away but stopped and said, "You know what? Yeah, I'd like that if the offer still stands."

Dean's face brightened again.

Chris took his coffee and made a gesture of thanks to the family before walking out of the store and going back to his motorcycle. He drank his cowboy and swallowed the bitter "goody powder." The vibration of his phone caused him to pause before cranking up his bike.

Are you alone?

Chris looked at the unknown number and replied, ?

This is Ca$h. Beau gave me your number. Call me. This is urgent.

Hey, Ca$h, what's going on?

How far away from Marcus's farm are you?

I can get back that way. Why?

There's been an accident, Preach, Ca$h replied.

Just as Chris started to respond and leave to make his way back to Marcus's farm, he heard the roar of maybe six bikes coming in from the main road. Chris's bike was parked on the other side of Dean and his family's van, which was blocking the riders' view of him. The riders filed into the store one by one, filling up the majority of the front. There were six Skulls lining the parking lot. However, they had not seen Chris yet, at least not as far as he was aware. Dean and his family came out of the store and walked right into the swarm of Skullys kicking down at the front doors.

"Well, what do we have here, boys?" one of the Skulls teased as Rebecca looked up from playing with her kids.

"You are one pretty little thing," another teased as the six bikers began surrounding her.

"Excuse me, but that's my wife. We are trying to leave," Dean said as he made his way through the men.

"I think I'll just take her home with me," one of them said as he pulled her close to his body.

Dean tried to defend his wife but was met with a hard right hit to the back of his head, dropping him to his knees. The children began screaming as they watched the men laugh while their daddy tried to get back to his feet. Rebecca began trying to fight her way to her husband, grabbing for her children at the same time. One of the bikers grabbed Rebecca's arm and pressed her up against the truck bed that was parked in the front space beside their bikes. She tried to resist him as the other bikers took their turns kicking and punching Dean while he frantically tried to get to his feet. The storekeeper left her position behind the register and grabbed the boys in an attempt to shelter them from the violence. The Skull that had Rebecca pressed into the side of the truck forced his lips to hers and began trying to get his hand up her flowered skirt.

Chris stepped in and attacked the man with a two-by-four, causing his hands to release Rebecca. When he was done, the man's body was lying on the pavement. He looked at Rebecca to be sure that she was unharmed and then turned his attention to the other five men. They all left Dean's body lying on the pavement and rushed to him. The first man felt the splinters of the two-by-four across his chest, and the second strike hit the back of his head. Chris positioned himself protectively between Rebecca and the remaining four men. He continued to move himself and Rebecca so that she was directly beside her injured husband, close to the safety of the store.

"You're gonna die, old man!" one of the men threatened Chris.

"I'm sure you're right. But not today," Chris responded. "Rebecca! Get Dean inside. Now!"

Rebecca tried to pull her lifeless husband to his feet but had no success. The driver of the parked truck, a seventy-year-old man, ran out onto the curb to help get Dean.

"We called nine-one-one!" the man yelled.

No one listened or seemed to care.

Chris was boxed in by the four bikers. The first Skull ran toward him, and he turned just as the man reached him. Spinning, the man using his forward momentum to redirect the attack, but Chris sharply thrust his forearm against the biker's jaw and throat. This sent the Skull backward, and he crashed into a curb with a loud thud. The next Skull was already rushing forward as his Brother crashed to the ground. Chris stepped into the biker's incoming right blow and crashed his forearms into him. He grabbed the man's right wrist with his left hand and pushed down on the elbow with his right elbow. He then struck the man's throat with his elbow, which sent his face straight into Chris's right knee.

The third Skull grabbed Chris from behind, and the fourth Skull rushed forward to attack. Chris jumped up and kicked the fourth biker's chest with both feet. This sent Chris and the biker holding him from behind backward into the wall of the store. The man released his hold, and Chris turned to face him. The man pulled a KA-BAR military blade from his pocket and began moving in and out of Chris's reach. Chris looked at the man. He was maybe in his early twenties.

"Son, you need to drop that blade before you need a really large Band-Aid," Chris said, half hoping the kid would do the smart thing.

The kid thrust forward, barely missing Chris's stomach. Chris reached into both of his blade sheaths and drew his own weapons. Before they were in his hands, the kid thrust forward again. His cold steel blade sliced through leather, cloth, and skin, opening up a wound on Chris's right pectoral. Chris had no time to draw his blades. The kid thrust again, but this time Chris parried the thrust with his right shoulder, checking the man's right side and striking him on the back of his right arm. The blade popped out of the biker's grip. Chris caught it and dug the weapon into the man's right shoulder.

"That's gonna leave a mark," he said.

He left the blade sticking out of the Skull's shoulder. The man immediately began screaming. Chris sent the man flying backward as he shoved his right heel into the biker's chest. The man lay motionless and unconscious on the ground.

Chris looked at the door of the store. The older man was armed with a Remington Pump 12-gauge shotgun and had it aimed at the five injured and unconscious bikers lying on the pavement in front of the store. Dean and his family, along with the store clerk, stood behind the door gaping, in awe of what had happened.

"You betta get gone, LoBo!" the old man said to Chris, who was trying to get out of his combat mindset. "You got to get, son! De cops, de are comin', son!"

Chris looked at the family in the window and the old man holding the 12-gauge.

"Go boy! I got dis!" the man yelled.

Chris headed to his motorcycle and hit the ignition switch, firing up his horse with an angry growl. He looked at the store and at Dean, who stood behind the store window, his hand on the glass. Rebecca was holding him up.

"Go!" Dean yelled, pointing toward the highway.

Chris looked and saw the sheriff's cars racing toward them.

"Go! Git out of here, LoBo!" the old man yelled.

The six bikers lay motionless on the ground. Chris twisted the throttle and disappeared behind the store, heading down a road that would soon bring him to Marcus's farm. The attack seemed like hours long, but in reality only a few minutes had passed since he received the text from Ca$h about Marcus.

"Please, God, if you're up there. Not Marcus," Chris prayed.

152

Chapter 26

Alibi

The sheriff patrol cars pulled in at the county-line store. They found the six Skull MC members lying face down, tied up with zip cords, in the old man's truck bed. Two of the men had suffered broken arms. One man still had a six-inch blade lodged in his flesh. He was lucky to be alive. The others had head wounds and injuries because of the two-by-four and the hard pavement.

"Anyone want to tell me what the hell is going on here?" the lead deputy asked.

"We got us sum brats with moto'cycles," the old man answered.

"Who is the one responsible for this mess?" the deputy asked.

"Well, see, dat depends on wat you want to call a mess."

"Mr. Floyd, what happened here?" the deputy demanded.

Dean walked out into the parking lot and said, "These men tried to harm my wife and Mr. Floyd, so I stopped them." He directed his attention to Mr. Floyd. "Isn't that right?"

"Are the two of you injured?" the deputy asked.

"Look at my face, Deputy. What do you think?" Dean said, trying to maintain his composure. "My kids have seen enough today. We are going home." He turned to shake Mr. Floyd's hand and looked into his eyes. "Thank you, sir."

Dean began walking to his van, where his family waited. He was halfway across the parking lot when he was stopped by another deputy.

"What happened to the seventh gang member?" the deputy asked. "Which way did he go?"

Dean looked at the deputy's name plate and politely said, "Deputy Nelson, I only counted six men. Not seven."

"I know—" the deputy began.

"Deputy Nelson! There were six," Dean said, looking directly into the deputy's eyes. "Are we clear?"

Deputy Nelson did not respond.

"Are we clear?" Dean said in a commanding voice.

"Yes, sir," the deputy replied.

Dean turned his attention to the ambulances and the EMTs working on the Skull MC members.

"Let me know if you need anything else," Dean said to Deputy Nelson.

"Yes, sir," the deputy answered.

Dean looked at the overweight deputy and, just to see his reaction, said, "Might be time for a diet, Martin."

Deputy Nelson gave no response.

"Are we clear?"

Deputy Nelson clenched his jaw and then replied, "I get it, sir," and walked off.

Dean waved at Mr. Floyd and got into his van with his family. Rebecca was still visibly upset. He took her face in his swollen hands and kissed her gently on her forehead as she sobbed uncontrollably. Their boys were huddled together in the backseat, but Dean told them to buckle up for the ride home. He and his family had now protected Chris's life, not knowing the full extent of their actions.

Chapter 27

Boot Laces

At the speed that Chris drove his bike, it looked as if it might shake loose bolt by bolt. His mind was racing with a combination of rage and concern. What did Ca$h mean by "an accident"? Roper Church was coming up fast. He turned down the road and headed to Marcus's farm. As he drew closer, he could see the smoke and flames rising from two bikes on the side of the road. The bodies of their riders lay face-first in the road. He slammed on his brakes and kicked down. He could see Marcus's farmhouse through the trees. The sound of gunfire echoed across the land. He made his way through the woods by foot without further hesitation. Marcus and Mrs. Ruth were in the house.

Just ahead, along the tree line on the left side of the house, he could see two bikers hiding behind a few rusted barrels that Marcus had used for burning in the past. One of the men was dressed in a solid-black BDU, and the other was wearing black jeans and a t-shirt covered only by an unmarked leather vest. They each had a Glock 9mm trained on the back porch of Marcus's home. The gun shots were coming from the front side of the house. These two men were strategically working their way to the rear and side doors. Chris was not carrying a firearm, but as always, he had his blades. He drew both knives from their sheaths and began moving quickly toward the men, making the least amount of noise as possible.

One is a probe. The other is a hired shooter, he thought.

He made his way through the trees, staying as low as possible. Once he reached the man in the BDU, he slipped in behind right lapel with his left hand, Chris made an expert cut under the man's trigger arm, causing the man to drop the gun to the

155

ground. Chris spun the man around and slammed his head into the trunk of a tree. The second man turned to fire his weapon at Chris but was cut short by a right fist to the jaw. The man began to fall back, but Chris grabbed him, crushing yet another skull to an innocent tree trunk.

He took both of their firearms and checked their clips. He hid one of them in the back of his pants and began moving down the same fence line that, only hours before, he and Marcus had walked next to, talking and drinking mugs of Mrs. Ruth's coffee. When he was near the sliding glass doors, a man came out of the woodshed, his firearm pointed at Chris. The man did not fire his weapon, though.

"Who gave the order to move in?" the man asked.

After staring blankly at the gunman for a second, Chris realized the man had assumed he was one of the bikers in the group. If the man was not a Skull, who was he? Why were they trying to get to Marcus? He put his back to the brown wood siding of the house. The stranger moved in, taking a similar position on the other side of the door. The mercenary was dressed in the same BDU as the other man in the woods. Chris mentally profiled him. The red boot laces and the bald head sparked something in his mind.

Vladimir, he thought.

"What's the move?" he asked, trying to get the man to assume leadership.

"We clear the house and wait for the Lobo to show up," the man answered.

"The whole club?" Chris asked.

"No, you idiot! Just the one they call Preach," he barked.

"Then what?" Chris probed.

The gunfire continued from the front side of the house. He heard whoever was shooting change from a sidearm to a rifle and then to a 12-gauge. That could only mean one thing: Marcus was running out of time. And ammo.

"You know this guy?" Chris asked

"We are getting paid to do a job! Do it, or go home!" the man barked.

Chris's mind shot back to Brownsville twenty odd years ago, when he had spoken the same words to the Kid.

"Copy that," Chris said as he moved toward the door.

The mercenary came up to Chris's side. The two men had their weapons ready to fire at the house.

"Hey," Chris said softly.

"Yeah?" came the reply.

Chris turned his weapon toward the merc's left leg and fired a single round into his step, causing him to fall forward, slamming his face into the concrete walkway near the deck. Chris secured his weapon. After removing its clip, he tossed it in the yard. The man grabbed his left knee where the bullet had made its mark. He looked up at Chris. Chris looked through the window and then back down at the merc.

"I'd suggest that you know your target," Chris said as he placed the clip in his pocket. "I'm Preacher, you idiot."

He took the earpiece from the man's ear and removed the receiver from his belt.

"Anyone know Cleo?" he asked into the set.

"Say it again, Echo three," came the reply.

"Echo three is no longer responsive," Chris said softly.

"Who is this?" the voice replied.

"The man who's gonna send you to hell. You should have never come after my Family," Chris said as he slowly opened the door, leaving the radio set behind.

He knew better than to rush into the house. Marcus was armed, fighting with an unknown number of bad guys. Chris knew that Marcus's main objective would be to protect his queen at all costs. He could hear Marcus trying to reload. There was no sound of Mrs. Ruth.

"'The Lord is my Shepherd...'" Chris whispered.

He reached the wall that separated him and Marcus. He put his back to it. He could hear Marcus speaking but could not tell what he was saying. He heard the front door crash open and the sound of footsteps rushing into the room. Marcus fired two rounds at the men. Mrs. Ruth began screaming. Chris knew that there was no time to hesitate. He dove through the doorway, firing his weapon at the men at the door. He rolled to his knee, firing two more rounds. Marcus and Mrs. Ruth were sitting behind her grandmother's grand piano, which was just behind Chris. Four men lay lifeless on the floor in front of him.

"Echo one... Echo two... Respond," the devices on their belts commanded.

Chris took one of the headsets and looked back at Marcus.

"All three teams are unresponsive," the voice said to a fourth party.

Chris tossed the spare clip to Marcus.

"I don't know who you are, but I will find you," Chris said into the mic.

He looked back at Marcus and Ruth.

"Can you get her to Steve?" Chris asked Marcus.

"Yeah, if you come with us," Marcus answered.

"Go! I'm right behind you. I'll cover your six," Chris said.

Marcus grabbed Ruth's hand, and they made their way through the backdoor. Chris followed behind, clearing the way with gunfire. He stayed back to cover them until they could get to the barn. He looked to the front and then to Marcus's garage.

"Preach! Get over here!" Marcus yelled as Chris disappeared past the side of the house.

Chris followed the wall of the house, trying to get to the garage without being seen. He checked the clip in the sidearm he had stowed away behind him. He had fifteen rounds in the clip, one in the chamber. He knew that the other weapon was close to empty. He checked. Five rounds left. He followed the standard rules of engagement. At least, all but one, as he had no battle buddy. However, he was used to doing things on his own. He needed no one. He was a "Ronin." A solo rider. He put his back to the wall and took a second to think before making his next move. Marcus and Ruth were secure. What was the "accident" Ca$h had told him about? The answer was already formulating, but his mind was not prepared to accept it.

Chris could hear voices in the front yard, to the right of the garage. Two, possibly three, men were scrambling to regain control of the situation. He had roughly twenty rounds left. If he underestimated the number of men out there, he would run out of rounds. Then he would be forced to improvise or surrender. Surrender was never an option. Rule number nineteen: "Neva tap." To surrender to any enemy was never an option. You prepared to fight until the end, even if it meant that you had to sacrifice your own life to save your Brothers. Chris feared nothing in this life. He knew that death was only the beginning.

His thoughts continued to race. He heard the footsteps of the men moving forward.

"Let's play," he whispered.

He turned the corner and spotted two of the armed offenders immediately. The first round caught both of the men off guard. He hit the man to his right in the knee, dropping him instantly. The second man raised his weapon to fire, but Chris shot him in the right quadriceps, dropping him, as well.

"Preach, drop the weapon!" a voice behind him demanded.

Chris turned to see a figure emerge from the garage. He was dressed in full body armor and had a masked face. His M1 was trained on Chris's chest.

"It's sort of funny that I get to kill you," the man teased. "The student becomes the master."

Chris looked at the man, and although he knew he had no way out, he looked beyond the man.

"Ca$h, you will never become my master," he said, his weapon at his side.

Ca$h played with the red laser dot on Chris's chest, moving it to his forehead.

"Should I take your head or your heart?" Ca$h asked.

Chris tried to put together a quick strategy. Nothing was plausible. Ca$h raised the weapon, preparing to fire. Just as Chris started to raise his own weapon to try and get in a Hail-Mary shot, something crashed through the aluminum garage wall, and he turned to see a blacked-out Humvee slam into Ca$h. His body flew through the air, slamming into the trees beside him.

"Get in!" Marcus yelled at Chris.

Chris jumped aboard.

Mrs. Ruth was lying on the back floorboard.

"It was a setup, Preach!" Marcus said as he handed Chris a clip.

"This has to end!" Chris said, looking at the main road. "You get what you put in, and people get what they deserve."

"I could tell you my thoughts, but I'm not sure you're ready to listen," Marcus said as he maneuvered "Steve," the Humvee, through the blockade of bikes.

"I'm not liking the way this could play out, Marcus."

"If God will bring us to it—" Marcus began.

"I just violated every law imaginable!" Chris said, cutting him off. "I just have to try and take as many of them with me."

"He will bring us through it," Marcus said as he focused on what was ahead of them.

"God isn't where I'm headed."

"You are wrong, Preach! He was in the pit with Joseph. He was there with Christ as He surrendered to the Cross," Marcus said, not looking at Chris.

They were headed to the only place they could think to go: the FARM.

"Marcus, they were all wearing—"

"RED SHOELACES," they exclaimed in unison.

They both looked at one another with knowing eyes.

"I'll call JT. We need to call an emergency Church meeting. Now!" Marcus said as he watched the road up ahead closely.

If Vladimir was in the states, that only meant one thing: The Butcher was with him. Chris and Marcus knew that their club Family was in grave danger.

Chapter 28

River's Edge

The last couple of days had become more complicated than Chris could have ever imagined. He had come back to Valley Town to figure out where the note had come from. Yet now he was once again involved in the dark web he had tried to escape. When he had left Valley Town, he had been certain that he would never return.

The only good thing that had come out of his trip home was the extra time he was spending with his son on the banks of the Desoto River. He enjoyed fishing and spending time with his boy. Storm was quickly becoming a man. It seemed like just yesterday, Chris was holding his little boy in his arms as an infant. Those days were special. Now, as Chris watched his son cast his line toward the fallen trees on the other side of the river, he recognized the strength in the boy who was turning into a man. Marcus had set up an emergency Church meeting later on, but right now his attention was on his sixteen-year-old son, who was standing next to him at the water's edge.

"Cast over toward the old dam, Son. Slow your pull and slightly flick your wrist as you reel in the line."

Just as he finished the last sentence, Storm's eyes widened in surprise as something hit his line. He began to reel in the line, the fish on the other end putting up a major fight. Chris watched his son fight with all he had to bring in what seemed to be a whale. Storm's excitement grew as the monster neared the bank. Chris sat back and laughed at the spectacle of his son landing the catch of the day. The fish continued to fight as Storm muscled it to the bank.

Chris stood up and grabbed the net to help bring in the fish. Just as he had the fish in the net, the weight and fight caught him off guard, and he lost his footing in the gravel and sand. He tried to steady himself, but it was pointless. He fell in. The water of the river felt like ice cubes. He hit the edge and was submerged to his chest. The net and the fish were still secure in his grip.

Storm was clearly fighting the urge to burst into fits of laughter after watching his father's body tumble head-first into the river.

Chris looked up at his son.

Storm looked down at Chris.

They both started laughing at the same time. The more they laughed, the harder they laughed.

Chris knew that this would be a special memory. He watched his son's laughter transform into tears. He felt peace. So much of Storm's life had been without Chris. He had tried being a father, but he had never really been given the chance by Storm's mother. So much time had been wasted.

No room for excuses, Chris thought as he pulled himself and the fish up to the bank.

"Nice catch, Storm," Chris joked. "You hungry? I need to get out of these clothes. We can go get wings. You up for that?"

"Yeah, Dad, whatever you want to do," Storm said.

"I think I'm in the mood for wings. What do you want to eat?" Chris asked his son, who was still chuckling.

"Can we go to The Belle?" Storm asked

Chris thought about it and looked at his son. He knew that part of the reason Storm wanted to go to The Belle was because it was part of his world.

"Let me call your mom. If she's okay with it, I'm good with it," Chris answered.

Chris was drenched and growing colder as they loaded the fishing gear into the small SUV. He dialed Storm's mom on his phone as he watched Storm busy himself. He was clearly hopeful that his mother would either not answer or, if she did, would give Chris permission.

"Hey, DG. Yeah, everything is fine," Chris said into the cell phone. "Storm and I are going to go get some wings at The Belle. You cool with that? If not, we can go elsewhere." He listened to the mother of his child on the other end. "Of course I wouldn't take him there without your consent."

Storm looked up at him and then back at the river.

"Sounds good. See you then," Chris said before hanging up.

He watched Storm closely. The boy was already accepting defeat.

"Where are we going to eat?" he asked in a disappointed tone.

Chris waited until he thought of the right response and then asked, "Storm, do you know what the LoBo rules are?"

Storm looked up at him and said, "I know what they are. I don't know them in order."

"The rules are not set up so that we're ruled by them. They are set up so that we can navigate through the journey with wisdom," Chris said to Storm as he changed his wet shirt and replaced it with a dry long-sleeved one.

Storm listened and continued to load up the cage.

"Rule number sixteen is to always communicate," Chris said. "Had I not kept the line of communication open with your mom, I could have possibly hindered the rest of my visit with you."

"So, where are we going to eat?" Storm asked sarcastically. "I know Mom said no to The Belle."

Chris finished changing into dry clothes and stood beside the rear hatch of the cage.

"Do you know what the ninth rule is?" he asked.

Storm looked at him and seemed to think about it, then said, "Yeah, it's to speak life.".

"Do you understand what that rule means?" Chris asked.

Storm looked down at the gravel under his boot.

"To be positive?" he answered under his breath.

"And what does that mean to you, Storm?"

"It means to not be negative," he answered.

Chris let out a hearty laugh and said, "Well, yeah. Something like that. It means to look for the best answer. Speak that instead of defeat. When you communicate with honesty and truth, you speak positive life into the atmosphere. You get positive results." Chris watched his son's eyes brighten. "When you are honest with the people you communicate with, they usually respond the way you desire them to. When they don't, you respect their wishes and regroup. But you will at least know that you followed the rules of engagement the best you could."

Storm looked at him, waiting for him to finish.

"You know how to get to The Belle from here?" Chris asked as he tossed the keys across to Storm.

"Yes, sir!" Storm said, unable to hide his excitement.

Storm took the driver's seat as Chris walked around to the passenger's side.

Chris looked down at his phone. There were a few texts from Rocky, and there was one from Marcus. They were concerning Church later that afternoon. He scrolled down the messages.

Hey, this is Preach. How's your day? he texted.

When they were a few minutes down the highway, his phone buzzed.

Hey, it's uneventful. Yours?

Want to get some coffee? he texted back.

I can't today. I'm babysitting my friend's kids.

Okay then. Maybe soon?

I'd really like that!

Chris smiled and sent back, Good. Me, too. Shoot me a text when you're available.

Okay, I will.

See ya later, Hannah.

Storm was driving in the seat next to him. How had his son grown up so fast? How had he allowed so much time to be wasted? He could only hope that would change soon.

As they drew closer to The Belle, Chris began wondering if this was a good idea. Did he really want to formally introduce his son to biker culture? He wanted his son to be a man, but he wanted his son to be his own person, not a copy of himself. They pulled into the parking lot, which was full of bikes.

"You stay close to me, Storm. If I go, you follow," Chris said sternly.

"Yes, sir."

"We clear?" he asked to confirm his position.

"You go, I go. Got it," Storm confirmed in his most serious "man" voice.

As they went through the doors of The Belle, Storm's eyes widened. He appeared to be captivated by every ounce of Chris's world. The Brothers and Sisters of the club immediately began welcoming him. They embraced Chris, their Captain of the Guard. Regardless of his leaving the club, he would apparently always be their leader, even if he chose not to continue. Storm enjoyed the attention. The Brothers teased him like he was already one of them. The Sisters began innocently flirting with him.

Chris felt awkwardness rise up within him. He did not want Storm to become part of what the club had become. He watched his son. He fought the idea of Storm being in this position. What was he doing? He loved the club—they were his Brothers, his Family—but he loved his son more. He knew how easy it would be for the club to pull him in. Storm was the eldest living son of the Captain of the Guard. Most of the club would follow Chris if he made the call.

"Storm, let's go," Chris said just as the waitress came to the table.

She was dressed in the sexy "uniform" of The Belle. Barely anything was left for the imagination.

"But, Dad—" Storm said as he looked at the barely dressed, and most likely barely legal, female standing beside him.

"Now, Storm," Chris demanded.

Storm was visibly disappointed but followed orders and headed toward the door. Chris handed the girl a folded twenty and headed to catch his son. Storm was standing outside next to the bikes.

"Storm, I know that you wanted to stay, and I know it doesn't make sense to you right now, but as your father, I can't put you in a position like this," Chris tried to tell his son.

"That's bull, Dad!" Storm yelled.

Chris felt anger and hurt.

"When you become a man, you can make your own choices. But right now, I'm responsible," Chris said, looking at his angry son. "Go on home, Storm. I'll see you before I head out."

He reached out to touch Storm's shoulder, but Storm pulled away and headed to the SUV.

"Don't worry about it, Dad," Storm said. "Just disappear again. I don't need you here."

Chris stood and watched his son slam the door and drive off in anger, leaving him brokenhearted.

I need a distraction, he thought.

Chapter 29

Distractions

Chris pulled out his phone and texted, Hey, Hannah, what would you like to eat for breakfast?

He headed into The Belle again and found his way to the bar.

"Irish breakfast," he said, not looking at the waitress.

His phone buzzed with a text that read, Umm…bacon??

You know it's the most important meal of the day, right? Chris responded, drinking his drink in one gulp.

"Another," he said, looking up at the bartender.

He reached into his cut and took out his cigar case. He removed a cigar, bit off the tip, and struck a match, savoring the coffee taste of his chosen cigar.

Is that right? What do you want for breakfast? Hannah asked.

Chris looked at the small crowd in the bar and then texted, You.

The phone went silent.

Chris knew that Church would be held soon, so he waited for Marcus to text him with the details of the meeting. He could feel the alcohol begin to affect his body.

DISTRACTION! his flesh screamed. NOW!

He waited on Hannah to text back, but it seemed unlikely.

A cute dark-haired waitress walked by the bar beside him. She looked up at him and smiled. Distraction located.

"Hey, how are you?" he said, smiling as he took in a long draw from his cigar.

"It's my second night. I'm tired, and the tippers here suck," she answered.

"What's your name?" he asked, not really caring.

"Becca," she answered, smiling.

"Nice to meet you. Around here, they call me Preach," he said as he took her hand into his.

She looked at him and then over at the bartender.

"The guy in that picture?" she asked, pointing at a picture just above the tip bell.

He looked at the photo of him, Marcus, the Kid, and Sammy.

"Yeah. It was a long time ago…but yeah," he responded. "When is your break?"

"I can take one now. Why?" she answered.

"Let's take a walk, then," he said as he squeezed her hand and led her to the front door.

She followed willingly, and they walked out of the bar, going past the barber shop and the tattoo parlor.

"How much do you make a night?" he asked.

"I only made thirty dollars tonight," she answered.

He reached into his cut and pulled out a roll of bills. He took three Benjamins and put them into her front pocket.

"You're mine tonight," he said, looking down at her.

"Okay," she said with a grin.

Chris desired to distract himself with as many pleasures as possible. Little did he know, the distractions were creating more of a mess and would lead to a craving to find more distractions. Crashing into a destructive wall would be the end result sooner or later. Right now, distractions led to pleasing his senses. Nothing else mattered. He had to hide the pain. Alcohol, drugs, and sexual adventures were his choices of entertainment. But by sunrise, the pain would be unmasked. The damage would linger. The hurt would remain unresolved.

After he had used Becca as his temporary drug, the two returned to the bar. She remained by his side the rest of the evening.

Marcus sent him a text message that read, They don't care. They say that Vlad and the Butcher are not their concern.

Chris looked at the text. If they weren't concerned about Vlad and the Butcher, then who were they concerned about? Those two had not emerged solely for Chris. He was sober enough to see that.

"Hey, Preach," said a girl with a broken voice who was standing beside his table.

Becca looked at the woman standing to Chris's left and scooted closer to him.

"Hey, Marla. How are things going?" he asked, looking away from her.

"Um…well, I came to see you. Is this your flavor of the night?" she asked, clearly trying to hide her hurt feelings.

Chris looked at Becca, then looked back at Marla and said, "Pretty good choice, wouldn't you say?"

"Are we still getting together later?" Marla asked.

He looked at her, then looked back at Becca and said, "Sure. Why not."

He blew smoke into the bar.

Marla gave Becca an evil grin and walked away after leaning in to kiss him on the cheek.

Becca pulled Chris closer and spat out to Marla, "Right now, he's mine."

Chris took a shot from the bottle of whiskey on the table and laughed. This mess was growing into small heaps of chaos.

Why are you doing this, Christopher? his mind asked.

He did not realize his answer was vocal when he said, "Because it hurts."

Becca looked at him and asked, "What hurts, Preach?"

He looked down at her, then back at Marla, who was walking to the ladies' room.

"Life."

It does not have to hurt anymore, Christopher, said the voice.

Chris looked back at Becca and asked, "What?"

She looked at him and repeated her question. "What is hurting?"

Chris was puzzled.

Hurting leads to healing, Christopher. But you cannot hide in the dark, the voice in his head said.

He took a long swig from the bottle and relit his cigar.

"I think I'm going crazy in this town," he said out loud.

This time, Becca paid him no attention.

His phone buzzed on the table in front of him, and the text from Hanna read, Are you okay?

He picked his phone up and texted back, Sure. I'd love to have some breakfast, though. :-)

There was a long silence again. Then the phone buzzed.

Come over Tuesday morning?

Chris smiled and responded, Absolutely.

I look forward to seeing you. Have fun tonight. I have you on my mind tonight... Not sure why.

Chris looked at the time. 19:00.

There is no limit, Christopher, the voice said.

Chris had had enough of the voices within. He took another drink from his bottle. Becca kissed his lips and excused herself to the ladies' room, so he tried to focus on the TV showing sports above him. Distractions were good. He tried to convince himself of the lie, and he tried to ignore the voice in his head.

This is only a season, son. I know it is dark. I know that it feels impossible. But remember, it is always darkest just before the dawn. This is only the beginning. I want you to know that you are closer than you have ever been before. It is not finished yet. It is only the beginning. Come home, the voice said slowly before drifting away.

"What the hell, Preach?" Marla said, pulling him from his thoughts.

Chris turned to look at her.

"Huh?" he asked, puzzled.

"Your little whore just came into the ladies' room to inform me that I had better back off from you," Marla said, tears in her eyes.

Becca stood in the background, her eyes on Chris and Marla's backs.

"Marla, she is just a distraction," Chris slurred.

She looked at him for a minute and then asked, "Is that what I am?"

Chris looked at them both and said, "Yes, Marla. I'm leaving town Tuesday night," before turning toward the TV again. He looked at them both one last time. "Both of you need to accept that you are my distractions. Enjoy the ride, or get off now. It's that simple."

Marla looked at him and then turned to walk away. She stopped as she passed Becca, and Becca turned to look at her.

"I'll win this fight, little girl. Back off before you get hurt," Marla warned.

"We will see who wins," Becca said, challenging her.

The dark clouds of the storm grew inside Chris's spirit. Something within him was calling him toward the open sky in the distance, away from the growing waves swelling around him. It was only the beginning.

Chapter 30

Cold Steel

"All I can see is that you failed," the man sitting in the shadows of the room said in a strong Russian accent.

"Someone was with him, sir," the suited man replied.

"I've seen the video! He was alone!" the man said violently as he slammed his fist onto the table.

"Sir—" the suited man tried to respond.

The man sitting in the shadows turned his chair until he was facing away from his subordinate and hissed, "Don't waste your worthless breath. You and your worthless men failed."

He stood from his chair and emerged from the shadows. He walked over to his desk and pressed a button to call his assistant.

"Get a cleaner in here," he said, looking at the man.

The fear grew in the man's eyes.

"Sir, I swear I will get the jo—"

Those were the last words out of his mouth. His body dropped to the floor. His eyes were wide open. His mouth was ajar. Once his body finished its descent to the hardwood floor of the office, his head rolled from his shoulders, stopping at the man in the shadow's feet.

"Now that's impressive," he said, laughing. "Evil... But impressive."

Behind the lifeless corpse stood a man wielding a long blade. He took a cloth from his pocket and wiped the blood from the cold steel. Expertly, he replaced the blade in the hidden compartment of the cane he carried.

"I have an unspoken rule about a lying tongue. Besides, I pride myself on the work I do," the man said.

172

Vladimir walked over to the man's body and kicked him in the ribs before saying, "He was a good soldier."

The mercenary didn't respond.

"Do you think you can finish the job?" Vladimir asked after his final kick to the man's body. He brushed what hair he had left on his head back into place and wiped his mouth with his handkerchief.

The mercenary looked at the balding Russian and said, "I can. But I want to know one thing."

"And that is?" Vladimir responded.

"Why do you want Preach dead?" he asked. "Not that it matters. I'll gladly cut him into pieces and feed his remains to hogs."

Vladimir looked at his hired assassin, smiled, and said, "Preach is in my way. The Lost Boys will follow him if he stands up."

The mercenary just listened.

"I want control of the money coming in and out of this pathetic hillbilly town. I want control of the drugs, alcohol, and weapons. I want the sex trade. I want it all," he said, looking back at the man.

The mercenary tapped his cane twice on the floor. He looked around the well-furnished office and walked over to Vladimir's bar. He opened a $1000 crystal bottle of Moscow vodka and poured two shots. He looked at Vladimir, then looked back at the bar. He opened an expensive cedar humidor that housed only the finest Cuban cigars and placed two of them in his jacket pocket.

Vladimir watched, and although he wanted to speak, he remained silent.

The mercenary walked over to his boss and offered him the shot glass.

"I will finish the job for you," he said. "But you need to know that I would recommend to you, as a professional, to let Preach do his mission. Let him focus on the Lost Boys and the Skulls." He tapped Vladimir's glass and gulped down the pure Russian water in one swallow. "You will lose a lot of men if you don't take my advice."

Vladimir took his own shot, put his hand on the man's shoulder, and said, "Comrade, do your job. I'll weigh the risk."

A knock at the door interrupted the conversation.

"What? What?" Vladimir yelled in aggravation, not taking his eyes off of the mercenary.

The door opened, and there were two men dressed in HVAC uniforms.

"Here to clean, sir," one of them said.

They wrapped the dead man's body in plastic. One of the men grabbed the head and placed it into a red bag. The other sprayed a cleaner on the floor, removing all traces of blood.

Vladimir looked at his henchman and said sarcastically, with no expression on his face, "You are THE BUTCHER. Kill him. Bring me his heart."

"If we stir up that nest more than your worthless men already have, Preach will not stop until you, Comrade Vlad, soil your ten-thousand-dollar suit, and he will leave you gasping for your last breath while he watches you go to hell," the Butcher warned.

"Not if you kill him first," Vladimir hissed in one breath.

The Butcher looked at Vladimir and walked out of the office without another word.

Chapter 31

The Hogs

The thick morning fog blanketed the field as the two men crossed over to the tree line. The strong odor of decay was unbearable.

"You better call the sheriff," the hunter said to his friend.

The two men stood looking at the gruesome sight before their eyes.

"Fire a shot into the mix of 'em."

The hunters raised their weapons and fired one round each, sending the boars away. The remains of what was barely recognizable as a human body lay before their boots.

"He doesn't have clothes on, Frank. Let's get out of here, man! Call Sheriff Roosevelt."

The two men headed back in the direction from which they had come, and Frank got out his phone and dialed.

"Hey, Betty, this is Frank Clifton. We found a body on my land." He stopped to listen. "Yeah, I'm being serious. The hogs had it. You need to get the sheriff and his CSIU out here. Tom and I are headed back to the truck."

Frank shut off his cell and said to his friend, "You go home, Tom. I'll wait on Bill and his boys to come."

He watched his friend drive away.

Chapter 32

Awakening

Chris woke up and checked his phone. He had received a text.

Hello, Mr. Caldwell. I need to speak to you as soon as possible. Please contact me at 706-657-7161.

He turned to look at the empty bed beside him.

Thank God, he thought to himself.

He reached down and picked up the shirt on the floor. He was still wearing his jeans from the day before. He stood, got ready in the bathroom, and then headed out the door. When he opened it, he found a basket with his clothes and his saddlebag. There was a note on the top that read, Hey, if you need or want me, I'm here. Love, M. He picked up his gear and dropped it on the bed. With his saddlebag in hand, he walked outside and found his abandoned motorcycle parked in front of the motel. The morning fog was thick in the air. He could hear the sounds of sirens racing down the highway, headed to the mountain roads out of town.

He pulled out his phone, checking it once more. The text that he had received earlier was swirling through his mind.

Dr. Collins? he replied to the anonymous sender.

Immediately, the phone buzzed.

Yes, Christopher. May we set up a meeting? It is most urgent.

I'm headed out now. Where? Chris texted.

Wally's.

Okay? When?

If it works for you, now, Dr. Collins responded.

En route.

Chris's bike roared under him as he started the engine. He pulled out of the motel parking lot and headed to town square.

The hum of speeding motorcycles tickled his ears as it got closer to his back tire. The first of the bikes pulled up alongside him. Lil Joe flashed a sign and backed up into formation. A staggered two-by-two formation followed the solo rider into town. Once parked, the other riders disappeared down the side roads surrounding Wally's. Chris spotted black SUVs in the lot. The two other bikes had parked on the other side of town square.

In the diner, Chris was greeted with a warm hug from Dolly. She whispered something in his ear.

"Cheers, Christopher," Dr. Collins greeted him.

"Yeah, yeah," Chris scoffed, removing his leather gloves and shaking Dr. Collins's cold hand.

Travis and another man sat at a side table. Travis nodded a greeting at Chris, and he returned the nod. Dolly brought him a fresh cup of coffee and walked over to the door, turning the OPEN sign to CLOSED. Chris watched but said nothing. Dr. Collins composed a message on his phone, and Chris silently sipped the hot coffee while observing his surroundings. Dolly vanished through the swinging kitchen door.

"We haven't been able to locate her since Friday night," a man to Chris's right said into his phone.

Travis stood up and walked over to where Chris stood against the counter. Chris stretched out his palm, and the two shook hands.

"What's the deal?" he asked.

"Dr. C felt it necessary to bring you up to speed," Travis answered.

"Who is missing, Trav?" Chris asked.

"We will let you in on all of it, Preach," Travis promised.

Chris was eavesdropping on Dr. Collins's conversation as he continued to interact with Travis.

"Mr. Caldwell is here. I'm about to sit down with him," Dr. Collins said into his phone. "Very unfortunate. Any idea how many? Is she among them?"

Chris turned back to Travis because if he had to ask him to repeat what he said, an awkward situation would surely arise.

"Who is missing, Trav?" he asked a little more aggressively.

Travis looked at Chris, then Dr. Collins, and said, "Preach, I give you my word. You will be told everything to the letter."

The kitchen door swung open. Four heavily armed men stepped forward and took their positions at the front door. One stayed planted at the kitchen door. Chris watched a group of men move into position outside the diner's doors. It was Sunday. The citizens of town were either still in their beds, recovering from the night before, or were planted in church pews throughout the county. The sight unfolding in front of Chris would go unnoticed by the eyes of the innocent and oblivious. Dolly had apparently closed the diner just in case a random sightseer dropped in for breakfast.

One of the armed men walked over to where Chris and Travis stood talking and politely said, "Excuse me, sir. The Bishop and his group are about to pull into the rear lot."

"Okay, thank you, son," Travis said.

Chris quietly watched and observed, muttering under his breath, "This better be good."

The kitchen door opened once more. This time, several Latino men in expensive suits entered. A small-statured man wearing a black suit with a purple priest collar stood in the center of their formation. The small man looked at Chris, and his eyes lit up like stars in the heavens. His men tried to stay in line, but he made his way to Chris.

"Oh, thank you, Father!" the man said as he embraced the reluctant biker. "I have looked forward to this day for such a long time."

"I assume you're Bishop Cruz?" Chris said, not really knowing what to say but trying to be respectful.

The man laughed as he continued to shake Chris's hand with both of his own.

"Gentlemen, maybe we should bring Christopher up to speed," Dr. Collins said.

The men sat down at a prepared table, and Dr. Collins looked around the room. Chris was the only man who remained uninformed in the current situation. An uneasy feeling began rising within him.

Dr. Collins began speaking to the group, saying, "Gentlemen, as most of us already know, Mrs. Dickerson's life has been placed under great danger."

Chris leaned forward, and his fists began to tighten.

"Last night, we secured her in a new location to better ensure her protection," he continued.

Chris looked at the men around him and exclaimed, "Who is missing!" before Dr. Collins could continue.

Travis tapped on the table to get Chris's attention.

"Who?" Chris said more powerfully. A hand touched his shoulder, and he looked up to see Dolly. "I'm not going to ask again, dammit!"

Dr. Collins glared at Chris and said, "Christopher, if you will listen, and I mean really listen, I will enlighten you."

"Christopher, God has orchestrated this meeting. Please rest," Bishop Cruz added in his thick Hispanic accent.

"The sheriff's department found remains on Frank Clifton's farm. They are not sure how many actual bodies there are, as the wild hogs had their way with them," Dr. Collins said.

"How many are they expecting?" Travis asked.

"At least three, but possibly more. Two male, one female," Dr. Collins answered. "We are concerned that a young lady— someone close to the people at this table—is among them, as she has been missing since Friday afternoon."

Chris listened. His heart began pounding. His fists clenched. Dolly squeezed his shoulder, and he looked up at her. There were tears in her eyes. The words that she had whispered in his ear when she'd hugged him made sense now.

"Please," she had whispered.

Chris scanned the room and asked, "Who do they have, and why?"

Travis answered the question that no one else wanted to answer, saying, "I think one of the bodies is Anna."

Chris looked up at Dolly and then stood from his seat and exclaimed, "Who has Anna Elizabeth!"

"Christopher, you do not realize it yet, but God has brought you home to free the community. It is with your knowledge and ability that we can bring an end to the chaos that came to Valley Town when you left," Dr. Collins said.

Chris picked up his phone and started to dial.

"Preach, I know this isn't easy, but you need to know that they also have Marcus," Travis said.

Chris's rage was growing, but he asked, "Mrs. Ruth?"

"We presume she's dead. We can't locate her," Travis said.

Chris could not breathe, but something inside him began to calm him down.

Do you trust me? the voice asked.

Chris shook his head, trying to ignore the voice.

Travis looked down at his vibrating phone, and his face changed.

"Jesus," he said as he slid the phone over to Chris.

The anger and the rage rushed through him.

Bishop Cruz broke the silence by saying, "In a dream, God told one of His saints that you would return to find the red rose. God called you 'la mano de Dios.'"

Chris looked at him and said, "I am not the hand of God, but I will find whoever has done this to my Family."

He looked at the picture on the phone, then picked up his phone and dialed.

"JT, I need your help. Cleo is lost," he said and then hung up.

He walked to the door. The group watched him as he grasped the metal handle.

He turned to face them and said, "I'm in, but we do this my way," and then he walked out, got on his bike, and sped down the asphalt, leaving the others behind in Wally's.

The image on Travis's phone needed no additional explanation. It had unleashed the beast within Chris.

Family, he said to the screaming voices in his head. He would find whoever was responsible for harming his Family.

180

Chapter 33

Empty Tank

Chris sped down the highway. The ghost riders filed into formation once again, with Lil Joe cruising alongside him. He nodded a greeting to his new shadows. Ahead, something caught his attention. The bell of the old church in the woods—the one right off Roper Road—was sounding the hour. 12:00. He turned and headed toward the old church, not really knowing why. Lil Joe and the riders followed. The bikes pulled into the parking lot one by one.

Lil Joe pulled up beside Chris and asked, "You okay?"

Chris looked at him and then at the church and answered, "I'll be back in a second."

He left Lil Joe and the others waiting on their bikes. He walked by the families leaving Sunday morning service. The pastor stood at the door, shaking hands and speaking to the congregation.

"Family" was not just blood. "Family" stood for much more than biology and genetics to Chris. "Family" was the benchmark of loyalty. He passed the sea of people and approached the altar. Kneeling, he prayed a simple prayer. The tears streamed down his cheeks as he looked up at the large cross hanging at the center of the wall.

"I'm sorry," he whispered. "I know that you don't give a damn one way or the other about me, but I sure could use your help. My Brothers need me. I'm going in against a force I've never seen before. I am alone. I have no one I can trust. If you don't help me, I will lose the only parts of life that I've ever known I can count on. Lord, I'm riding on an empty tank here, and I don't know what else to do."

Chris knelt there for a moment, waiting. He was unsure what he was waiting for and why he was waiting. He was searching. Hoping. There was nothing but silence.

"Okay then. I'll do it my way," he said, growing angry, and stood to leave.

The pastor of the little church was leaning on an empty pew a few feet away.

"Can I help you, son?" he asked.

Chris looked at the elderly man wearing jeans and a black button-up shirt. The shirt was untucked, the sleeves rolled to his elbows. He studied the man for a minute, trying to place him in his memory.

"Are you the pastor of this church?" he asked.

"Yes, sir. My name is Apostle James Wallaby," the man responded.

Chris laughed and shook his head, saying, "You church people are more like bikers than some of my club members are."

The pastor looked at Chris and laughed, then asked, "And why is that?"

"Because you're all focused on titles," Chris mused.

The pastor looked at the floor and smiled, seeming to remember something, as well.

"Well, how about this? I'm Jimmy. It's nice to meet you."

Chris looked at him again while glancing at the exit.

"I'm Christopher Caldwell," he said and then began laughing again. "Most of the people around here call me—"

"Preacher," the pastor said, cutting him off.

"Yeah. Preacher," Chris said, realizing he had sounded judgmental with his earlier comment.

The pastor reached out to shake his hand, and Chris was surprised when he gave him a club shake instead of a common civilian shake. He looked at him, puzzled.

"Why do they call you 'Preach'?" the pastor asked.

"I caught the nickname in my teens. A lot of people have their ideas or have listened to myths. But I got the name from a traveling minister who was trying to get me to go to Lee University

182

instead of—" Chris began explaining, but he cut himself off when it hit him.

He looked at the pastor again. He had known the man looked familiar.

"An evangelist named Jimmy Wallaby came and held a revival. He gave me the nickname," he said, realizing the man standing there was Jimmy Wallaby in the flesh.

Chris had bucked the ministry calling and had chosen to leave for the Army. He'd lived a life as a mercenary and a renegade instead of taking Jimmy's advice and pursuing ministry. The nickname had stuck because he had received letters from "James Wallaby" during boot camp, and Scriptures were always written on the envelopes.

"How are you, Preacher Man?" the pastor asked. He looked at the cross behind Chris's head and smiled. "Your mama came here a lot before she went home. We miss her smile. She helped change this church."

Chris fought his emotions and, instead of mentioning his mother in turn, said, "I'm good, sir. I'm sorry if I was rude. I'm struggling, and God has abandoned me in the field to die alone."

"Son, one thing that I'm absolutely positive of is that God has not done such things," the pastor responded.

Chris looked at the floor and fought back his emotions once more as he replied resentfully, "He left me a long time ago, Pastor. He left when He took my mom."

Pastor Jimmy started to comment but was not given the opportunity.

"It was good to see you again. I have to go. This was a waste of precious time," Chris said as he stormed out of the church and went to his awaiting escort.

***

Pastor Jimmy watched him leave and walked to the altar, where he took a knee and began to pray.

"Father, you are the creator of the universe. You, Lord, opened the way for your children to cross through the Red Sea, and you parted the waters of Jordan for them so they could leave the wilderness. Father, you are a sovereign God. Your church needs you. Today, one of yours came seeking your protection. He has already stepped out in faith, trusting in your beloved Son's finished work on Calvary, even though he seems lost at the moment. Lord, I pray that you send ministering angels to watch over and protect Christopher. I pray that you send members of your Church to minister him in a way that only you can provide. Lord, I fear that whatever his struggle is, it may be more than he can handle without your grace.

"Your Word says, Lord, in the book of Isaiah that no weapon formed against us shall prosper. And it teaches us that no matter what, you, Lord, will never leave us or forsake us. The cross of Christ finished the redeeming work. And He has your Holy Spirit dwelling within Him. Lord, build up an army of your warriors and bring forth a powerful revival here in Valley Town again.

"Lord, we are in need of warriors who will boldly stand up and proclaim Your Word in the face of anything hell sends our way. Warriors who remember that no giant, no mountain, and no circumstance is ever going to be bigger than you, Lord. Let us be warriors on our knees, worshiping you with our whole hearts, teaching the world around us that your salvation is real and that all we have to do is call on the name of your beloved Son, Jesus Christ. Thank you for sending Him to die so that we may live. We do not deserve it, but He gave it freely. I pray this in the name of Jesus Christ, the Messiah! Amen!"

After Pastor Jimmy finished praying what he thought was a private, quiet prayer, he finally stood and opened his watering eyes, only to find that he had been very vocal. When he stood and turned around, he found eight members of his church family kneeling in prayer with him. Their eyes were still closed. Some of them had their hands raised toward heaven. They were all praising and worshiping the Father in their own ways. They

184

were praying with their pastor, hoping for the same things he was. Pastor Jimmy raised his hands again and began praying over the warriors knelt down before God.

"Father! Look at this!" he exclaimed with overwhelming emotion. "You promise us that when there are two or more gathered together, you are with us. Father, we seek your deliverance, your salvation, your healing, your protection, and your provision to accomplish the tasks that you have set before us."

After he looked at the men, the women, and the few teens who bowed before the King of Kings, he began to sing.

"'Amazing Grace, how sweet the sound, that saved a wretch like me.'"

The others joined in with their pastor.

"'I once was lost, but now I'm found, was blind but now I see.'"

Pastor Jimmy raised his voice toward heaven once more as the others continued the hymn.

"So clearly, Lord! So clearly!" he said as tears ran down his cheeks.

***

Chris's hurting, painful, and angry prayer was the beginning of something greater than a hurt man's prayer as he shook his fist toward heaven. Something in the atmosphere was changing. Chris had not known why he was drawn to that little country church in the woods, but it was for a reason. Life was about to change for everyone in Valley Town.

Chapter 34

Thirteen Roses

Chris and his ghost escort drew near the bridge that crossed the county line. Considering recent events, it was quite possible that there would be a spotter located on the other side of the next hill. Although he was unsure of Lil Joe's loyalty, there was no time to test his suspicions. Lil Joe was the only option. Lil Joe pulled up beside Chris and patted his chest twice before pulling back. He and his men turned around, heading back into town. Chris understood the gesture and acknowledged Lil Joe with a similar signal, then sped ahead over the hill, disappearing over the horizon.

Just as expected, on the other side of the old bridge, a utility van was parked facing the direction of the FARM. Two probates sat inside smoking and playing cards as they watched the roads for any sign of trouble coming toward the FARM. Chris sped past them, flashing a specific hand signal. In other words, a number one with only the middle finger, popularly known as "the bird." One of the probates grabbed his phone and sent a text to the FARM's sentry guards, letting him know that a Brother was coming.

Chris pulled into The Belle's parking lot and backed into a spot. He acknowledged the two sentries who revealed themselves on the building's tower, then made his way into the pub.

Sundays at The Belle were rarely busy, and tonight was no different. Only five or six townies lingered at the bar, and a few stragglers hogged the pool room. The jukebox was playing an old Willie Nelson hit. It was dead inside. Typical Sunday.

Becca came out of the pool room, noticed Chris standing at the front, and hurried to greet him.

"Hey, Becca," he said, trying to pry the girl from his grimy clothes.

She looked up at him and flashed a smile, showing that she was happy to see him.

"Did you come to see me?" she asked in excitement.

He looked around at the room and then down at her and answered, "No."

He headed to the kitchen doors that would lead him to the clubhouse hidden in the heart of the FARM's compound.

She watched him leave, just standing there, her heart and emotions on her sleeve. His words had hurt her deeply, but she knew the rules. She was not a Sister. Becca was only a waitress at The Belle.

Chris made his way across the courtyard and headed to the clubhouse. The men inside turned to scan him as he entered and headed straight toward the office where JT was.

"Preach! Hold up. I have to search you before you go in," Beau said, standing and looking at Chris.

Chris stopped where he stood, raised his arms, and said, "Well? Come on," submitting to the security protocol.

Beau ran the wand across his body, and Chris pulled his cut open, displaying his blades and the weapon in his rear holster.

"Take care of my ladies," he said to Beau.

Beau put the firearm in his own waistband and took the blades to the bartender.

"We good?" Chris asked.

Beau looked at him humbly and nodded his head.

Chris walked over to the door, knocked, and walked in, getting JT's attention.

"Hey, Preach. What can I do for you?" JT asked without taking his eyes off the multitude of TV screens showing videos from the side rooms in the clubhouse.

Each screen had a different scene playing live. All of them were recorded, and some went straight to the Internet. Chris had seen them before, and he was not impressed.

"You come to tell your President goodbye?" JT said, clearly trying to provoke Chris.

Chris wanted to shove his fist through JT's skull but chose to control his temper for the sake of Anna Elizabeth, Marcus, and Mrs. Ruth. He only knew for sure that one of them was still alive, and that was because of the pictures that Travis had shown him back at Wally's.

"JT, I need to know what's going on. Someone has Marcus and his wife," Chris said as he watched JT slowly turn in his chair.

"First of all, Preach, there's nothing about club business that you are privy to right now. So, you don't need to know anything," JT snapped.

Chris started to reword his statement but was interrupted.

"I don't care about that old man and the old Mexican whore he married," JT said with a grin, obviously knowing that his words would bring the rage out in Chris.

Chris's fists clenched as words poured from JT's rotten-toothed mouth, but he remained calm.

"What about Cleo's daughter? You care about her, you son of a bitch?" he asked.

JT seemed to want to spout out another derogatory comment but chose not to this time. He most likely knew Chris's next move. Any statement contradicting Chris's question would be met with a call of arms by the club. Over the years, even the members who did not completely understand its meaning to the fullest knew that "Cleo" was the heartbeat of the club itself. JT looked out at the dozen or so members who stood there and tried not to watch the two men arguing.

Beau had overheard the last statement Chris had said. He walked closer but didn't come all the way to where Chris stood.

"They have three people I love, JT," Chris said, looking out into the common area.

"All that I need to know is who you pissed off and who thinks I might be back as a wraith," Chris continued. "It would be nice to have the club's help, but if not, I'll go solo."

188

JT looked at Chris and the men now walking toward the two officers of the club.

"Ivan made the call last week, when you first got here, that sent Vladimir and his henchmen to the Valley," JT said, confirming what Chris was already thinking. "They think that you have returned to take my place as president."

Chris looked out at the men behind him and said, "I didn't come for you or the club. I came to find out who sent me this."

He pulled out the note and displayed it for JT to see.

Beau held back no longer.

"Preach, I'll go with you," he said, looking at JT.

The rest of the men all stood with Beau. Each man offered aid for his Brother.

Chris looked at JT and said, "I'm not here for your seat, JT. But I can't leave until one of our Brothers, his wife, and Anna Elizabeth are safe. Like you, I've sworn an oath to protect my club, my Brothers, and those connected to the club."

JT looked at the Brothers and wrote an address on a sticky note, handing it to Chris.

"Go with my blessing and use whatever you need from the club," he said loud enough for the others to hear.

Chris took the note while Beau and the others filed in behind him. They made their way to the firing range and the club's armory. When the men entered the armory, they found Sammy sitting in a chair.

"Hey, Sammy, I need Thirteen Roses," Chris said, knowing that his old friend would understand its meaning.

Sammy grabbed the phone at the desk, and when someone answered, he began the process.

"Done. Rocky is looking for war wagons," Sammy said, standing up.

He walked over to a side door and unlocked it so Chris could enter solo. The other men waited as Chris and Sammy spoke privately.

"You know what I need from you, Sammy," Chris said. "We have to do this with secured lines. Sammy, I can't let Anna Elizabeth die."

Sammy looked at him before saying, "I'll run the Alpha team. You take the Charlie team. And I'll get an LS to organize the Bravo team."

"Rocky?" Chris asked.

Sammy smiled and answered, "You betcha."

Chapter 35

MIA

"Hey, Rockhound, we just got a call from Cruz's people," a young man said as he knocked on his president's clubhouse door.

Rockhound glanced away from his video screens, hardly acknowledging the Skully standing by the door.

"And?" he asked in an aggravated tone.

The young member tried not to stumble backward because of his fear. The angry tone was now being on him.

"I have Cruz on the phone now, sir," he said, handing Rockhound the phone with shaking hands.

Rockhound snatched the phone out of his hand and slammed the door, almost catching the man's arm as it shut.

"Hola, Señor Cruz," Rockhound muttered, attempting to speak as much Spanish as he could.

His eyes grew larger as he heard the man's voice in the receiver.

"Mr. Saunders, you promised to meet the deadline on my product. I am not looking at a truck on my property," Cruz said.

Rockhound began to speak but was cut short.

"EXCUSES!" Cruz screamed. "If I desired childish excuses, I would go play at St. Andrew's Orphanage. I want what you promised me."

The call ended.

Rockhound hung up his phone and closed his eyes for a brief moment before dialing.

"You got my voicemail. Do what you do," said the voice on the other end.

Rockhound's anger grew more intense.

"Rick, I've been calling you for two days. Where are my guns?" he said into the phone with almost no emotion.

He hung up, opened the door, and walked to the clubhouse bar to put the phone back in its unit.

"Eighteen hundred hours," he said to the barely dressed female behind the bar.

She quickly poured the shot and placed it on the bar in front of him. He drank the tequila and shifted his eyes until they were focusing on the ceiling. He noticed that the young member who had delivered the phone sat at the bar and was looking up at the screens. He turned to face him, leaning on the bar to seem relaxed.

"Yolo, have you seen Rick?" he asked, smiling.

The young man looked at his leader and thought about the question. He thought a little bit longer than Rockhound liked. Rockhound used his right hand to backhand the kid, sending him flying off of his stool and onto the floor, where he quickly received a boot to his ribs.

"Mouse?" Rockhound said, looking at the girl behind the bar.

Her hands were covering her own mouth as she seemingly tried not to scream.

"Yes, sir?" she struggled to answer.

"Have you seen my son?" Rockhound asked, smiling.

She quickly responded by shaking her head no.

He removed the 9mm from his pants and placed it against Yolo's left temple.

"I'll try this again," he said, looking around the room at the half dozen or so members now watching the scene take place. "Has anyone seen my son?"

All of the people in the room shook their heads no.

"You mean to tell me that out of five members of my crew, four of whom happen to be his groupies, have yet to see him!"

They all answered no once again.

Rockhound looked around the room again and tucked the firearm securely into the back of his pants. He reached down to grab the injured biker's arm and help him up. The young man shrieked in pain as he was forcefully lifted to his feet. Rockhound motioned for the girl to pour another shot. He slammed it and then carefully placed the glass back on the bar. Without warning, he shoved his boot heel into the young man's chest, sending him flying across the room. The man landed in a painful curled-up position and was fighting to breathe.

"Find him," Rockhound said as he walked back to his office. "NOW!" he screamed, sending everyone in the room into a frenzy.

He looked at the kid curled up on the floor.

"Take him to the ER," he said as he shut the door behind him.

Once inside his office, Rockhound placed his hands on the desk and looked up at the multitude of video screens that displayed every sexual perversion imaginable.

"Where are you, boy?" he whispered as he bowed his head.

Chapter 36

Blueprints

Chris looked up at the clock hanging in the armory's office. The time read 21:00.

"Is that clock right?" he asked Sammy, who was stretched out in a recliner.

Sammy looked at the clock and then at his watch and responded, "Yeah, it's nine p.m. Why?"

Chris looked back at the clock and then back at the desk full of floor plans.

"Sunday?" he asked, puzzled.

Sammy looked at him and laughed.

"Lil Brother, you have been at it for almost twenty-four," he said as he got up to pour Chris some coffee. "You want a cigar?"

Chris looked at the clock and sat back in the chair. Sammy poured the coffee in his cup and laid a Cuban cigar on the desk in front of him. Chris picked up the cigar and lit a match, inhaling the aroma of the high-quality Havana.

"You have the roses ready?" he asked Sammy.

"Yes, Preach, everything is in motion," Sammy answered as he sat back in the recliner.

Chris picked up his cell and sent out a text.

Hey, gal, how are you?

He sat the cell back down and sipped his coffee. His eyes looked up at the clock again and then back at Sammy.

"Twenty-four hours? It's Monday?" Chris asked in a daze.

Sammy looked at his old friend and said, "Lil Brother, go get some sleep."

Chris looked at the plans again.

"Go, Preach," Sammy demanded. "We can't move right now anyway. You know that."

Chris's cell buzzed, indicating a text.

You still coming for breakfast? Hannah responded.

Chris smiled and looked through the photos on his phone. He chose a funny picture that he had found a few days before. It showed two lovers in bed. The caption read, Breakfast, the most important meal of the day. He sent the photo with a smiley face.

Sammy got up from his recliner and began putting the plans and diagrams into a folder.

"Go," Sammy said again.

Chris looked at his friend and took a draw from his cigar, and Sammy walked over to the door and looked back at him.

"Go! Before I shove my prosthetic up your rear," Sammy joked.

Chris looked down at his cell.

Can't wait, was her reply.

Chris grabbed his jacket and headed out the door. As he began walking across the courtyard, he heard the sound of heavy metal music coming from The Belle. He changed his direction and headed to the rear entrance of the pub. The crowd was light. The music was loud and angry. There was not a Brother anywhere to be seen. This was exactly what he wanted. He made his way to the horseshoe bar. The bartender placed a drink in front of him without a word. Chris looked at the drink and then at the bartender.

"Irish breakfast. Two ounces of Jamey and one ounce of butterscotch over ice, topped with fresh orange juice," the man said as Chris took a sip.

Chris nodded his approval and satisfaction. He scanned the room, which was lightly scattered with townies and groupies of the band playing covers from the eighties' best heavy metal bands.

"Hey, baby," Marla said as she touched his arm.

"Hey, Marla," he said as he looked into the pool room. "Have you seen Becca?" he asked, knowing the question would hurt Marla's feelings.

"Yeah, she's in the back. You want me to go fetch her?" Marla snapped back.

Chris could not help but grin as he laughed and said, "Fetch?"

Marla looked at him with a jealous glare and said, "That's what you do with bitches, isn't it? Have them fetched?"

She started to walk off.

"No, Marla, I'm sorry. I was trying to razz you," he said.

She looked at him, clearly still hurt by his games, and said, "It worked," before walking off.

He finished his drink and put a twenty on the bar. He knew it would be best to leave before causing more of a mess.

His thoughts were on the blueprints that had been spread in front of him for so many hours, and he was also thinking of the choices he had made since he came back.

These blueprints are leading you to destruction, Preach, he thought to himself.

He crushed his half-smoked Cuban and headed to his room in the clubhouse.

Chapter 37

Breakfast

The alarm clock buzzed off of the dresser next to Chris's bed, hitting the floor with a loud thud and waking him from a deep sleep. He had fallen asleep before 22:30, and the time now was 07:00. Eight hours seemed like eight minutes, but he was fully rested. He grabbed his saddlebag and headed for the shower. The hot water on his naked body felt liberating. The soreness from the past several days was seemingly nonexistent. He headed out of the bathroom and made his way down the hall, heading for the common area of the clubhouse. A door opened to his right, and Marla exited with just a towel wrapped around her.

She looked at Chris with a devilish grin and said, "Hey, baby."

Chris kept moving forward and said, "Hey, Marla. Tell Becca good morning."

Marla looked at him and then back into the room she had stepped out of. Becca's naked body lay on the bed, waiting for Marla's return. Marla's scheme was failing. She watched Chris exit the hallway. She stomped her feet in a childish fashion and went back into the room with Becca.

Chris stopped at the clubhouse bar and poured himself a cup of coffee as he sent a text to Hannah.

Good morning, beautiful. I need your address.

A few moments later, she responded, 251 Daisy Circle.

He almost spit his coffee.

The gate code is 4920#.

Chris could not believe what he was reading.

Headed your way, he responded.

He finished his coffee and headed out the door.

What are the chances of that? he thought.

Hannah's address was five doors down from his old townhome.

He drove down the highway and pulled into the gate, pressing the numbers on the pad in the security box. The large iron gates opened, letting a stranger into the closed neighborhood. He pulled into Hannah's driveway and walked up the sidewalk to the door. She answered the door wearing a pair of black boy shorts. The small shorts exposed her beautiful muscular legs, and the thin white t-shirt revealed her sculpted abs. Chris entered the cinnamon-and-vanilla-scented townhome. Hannah walked over to her kitchen, and Chris watched her body move in front of him. She stopped and turned to look at him.

"Coffee?" she asked.

He smiled and then shook his head in affirmation.

She poured them two coffees, and they walked over to her red sofa. She sat Indian-style on top of the comfortable cushions. He sat down on the other side, facing her. They sipped on the hot liquid for a while, and then she stood to return to the kitchen. He stood up as he watched her walk by him. He gently took her arm in his hand, and she looked up at him. She turned to face him, and he pressed her body against the wall separating the living room and kitchen. She looked up at him as he took her face in one of his hands and leaned in to kiss her lips. His other hand traced her back and found no bra. Their passion grew stronger and hotter, her hands on his chest and arms. She reached down to unbuckle his belt, but he withdrew, pulling her to the sofa. She lay back on the cushions as he peeled off her shorts, exposing her shaved body. She was sexy, beautiful, and intoxicating. He kissed her lips once more before getting on his knees between her legs. The passion, desire, and intensity grew as they enjoyed each other. When it was over, they both collapsed on the floor in exhaustion, gasping for oxygen. They lay there for a while, her head on his chest, his arms around her athletic and well-toned body.

She looked at his watch and said, "I have to go to work," as she stood up from the living room floor.

Chris watched as her naked body walked into the kitchen and came back with a bottle of water.

"You want to shower with me?" she asked.

Chris heard her words, but they did not register. He was enamored by the sight in front of him.

She laughed and said, "Hey, Mr. Cosmo. Do you want to take a shower? I have to get ready for work."

They gathered their clothing, and she led him upstairs to her bedroom. She was facing away from him as she stood next to the bed. He could not take his eyes off of her. He walked over, standing behind her, and she leaned against him. Their chemistry was undeniable. It was as if they had known each other a lifetime. He kissed her neck and her lips again. She leaned over the bed and reached to guide him inside her from behind.

"You have to hurry this time," she said, moaning in pleasure as he began stroking.

Moments later, she was shaking from her orgasm just as he finished. She left him lying on the bed to go turn on the water. He walked to the bathroom and entered the steam and hot water beside her. They kissed passionately again. She looked up at him and smiled. He could tell that she wanted to say something, but he was not going to ask or push. They dressed and headed downstairs to leave. As she locked the door behind her, she turned and put her hands on his leathers.

"I'm not stupid, Preach," she said.

Chris looked down at her, listening to her words.

"I know you have others. Just don't hurt me," she asked of him.

He did not respond. He knew he was in over his head. She was different. He could feel the connection, and it scared the hell out of him.

She kissed him goodbye, and he watched as she drove off. He looked at his cell phone to check the time. 11:00. He had arrived at 08:00. He scanned through his missed calls and texts. As he was scanning, she sent him a text.

I hope, I hope, I truly hope that I see you soon.

You will, he replied.

Her response was simple: :-P

It made its point, and Chris smiled at her seemingly innocent yet dangerous personality.

He looked back at the other texts. The one from Sammy caught his attention.

Bravo has intel.

Chris hit "call back."

"Talk," he said when Sammy answered.

Chris's focus changed. There was a time to play and a time to work. Now was the time to work.

Chapter 38

Collision Course

Chris kicked down and scanned the area before dismounting his bike. To the right was a large patch of pine trees, and just past them were the open fields that produced corn until the fall harvest. To the left of the road was a trail of rocks leading up the mountain. Just ahead, a small group of old farmhouses sat quaintly. The house of interest had smoke rising from its chimney. He hooked his helmet on the handles of his bike and headed up the tree line toward the farmhouses. Rage and hate rushed through his veins.

Control your emotions, or lose your vision, said the voice deep within him.

The photographs that Travis had shown him ran vividly through his mind. He was unsure of what he would do once he found the person, or people, responsible, but one thing was set in stone: They would pay deeply. He reached the home with the burning fireplace and hesitated, thinking about his next move. He instinctively circled around to the side so that he would not be noticed from the windows. So far, nothing out of the ordinary. But he knew what was coming next would be a turning point in his life forever. He moved in ways that kept him hidden from both the farmhouse windows around him and the road coming in from the main highway.

He considered this whole situation grimly. The men that he would find inside this house had served him loyally since the conception of the Lost Boys. He had no doubt that they held the keys that would unlock the answers he needed in order to find his mentor. He once again assessed the situation, and his eyes darkened. Maybe he would find answers from loyal friends, but he knew the odds were not in his favor.

As he turned the last corner of the house and headed up the backside, moving to the rear patio, he could hear the voices of two men standing on the patio's edge. Their dialect was foreign, either Romanian or Slovakian, but from this angle he could not understand. This was not good. He dropped to a knee so he could crawl underneath the patio and get a better angle. He looked around the bottom of the patio to find the men's location.

"Always quick to turn on a Brother," a third man said as he walked out of the house to join the other men.

The words sent chills up Chris's spine, as he recognized the man's voice. He drew his firearm from its holster and readied himself. He reached a spot directly underneath the men. Silent in the darkness under the patio, he listened to the mixture of English and what he was now certain was Slovakian.

"They want us to hit the old man's ranch, which should lure Caldwell out into the open," one of the men said.

"Looks like he isn't hiding too hard," another responded.

"What's that supposed to mean?" the first asked.

"Preach hasn't rode with a group since he got here, and he hasn't been shy about being seen in public. He took those Skullys down at the QT robbery, and everyone knows that was him who stepped in to protect the Crandall target on Highway Eleven. He made a mess of things without trying to hide too hard. That's all I'm saying," the man fired back.

"All I know is that Mr. C wants his head in a box," one of the others added.

"Well, that's our job. But I wouldn't be so excited about going in. When he finds out about Marcus and the girls, I'm not so sure things will be in Cruz's favor," one added.

Chris wanted to fire his weapon and take the men above him out, but he knew that he had to slip back out and head to what they just called the "ranch." He knew that any movement would put him right into their hands.

What if I'm wrong? Chris wondered. They want me to poke the hornet's nest. But I must be smarter than the hornet.

In his heart, he knew that it was the only way. These men already had Marcus, Ruth, and Anna. Plans and actions had already set chaos into action. He knew that he had to make sure his choices were on the mark, or he would allow emotion to blind him and make costly mistakes.

He'd heard enough. He slipped out, making his way back up the tree line to his bike. His rage grew stronger.

Control your emotions. Do not chase the rabbit into the wrong hole, he thought.

The course was rocky, and he knew that he was headed toward a head-on collision with something unknown and very dangerous. He had no other choice.

Chapter 39

The Unknown

Chris's emotions were fighting for control. He was upset about the pictures Travis had shown him and the words he had heard at the old safe house, but his inner voice kept trying to keep him calm. He knew that the voice was right. To run into battle full of emotion of any type was not wise.

Do not chase the rabbit, Chris, he thought.

He knew that they had to move on the situation soon. By now, Mac, Beau, and Sammy had their teams ready. Rocky and the loyal Sisters would be ready to work their magic.

Please, God, he thought as his thoughts turned back to Marcus and the girls.

He knew that he was running out of time. He pulled his bike over in an old shopping center and retrieved his cellphone, making a call.

"Gabriel, I need you to get your gear ready to roll," he said into the receiver.

"Okay, boss, what's going on?" Gabriel responded.

"We have an unknown threatening the safety of our Brothers and Sisters," Chris said.

"Say no more," Gabriel replied.

"Gab, be careful, son."

"Will do, Preach."

"I love you, Gabriel."

"Preach, it's gonna be okay. But I love you back," Gabriel said, seeming to try to reassure Chris.

"I am my Brother's keeper," Chris began.

"And my Sister's protector," Gabriel concluded.

Chris hit the "end call" button and noticed a few missed texts. He scrolled down the page, looking at the messages.

Marla: Hey, Preach, can you call me, please?

Sandy: Need you to call me.

Mac: Ready to roll.

Hannah: TOY :-)

Chris looked up from his phone, trying not to smile, but it was pointless. His mind was intoxicated by something strange, something that was growing stronger, and if he wasn't careful, it would change him. He just wanted to get out of this town. He had not returned for compilations. He's come back to solve a puzzle, but the longer he was in Valley Town, the more he got sucked into the wastelands that he had left three years prior.

He looked down the highway.

The Lost Highway, he thought to himself.

Everything had changed since he left. His club and the townies. But most of all, it was he himself who had changed. The longer he had been gone, the more separated he had become. He was separated from more than just the club and this small town. He had cut off his emotional triggers. Murphy had been a refuge, but it had allowed him to hide from everything he had ever known, mainly himself.

He hit "dial" on his phone.

"Hey, Brit," he said as the voice on the other end picked up.

"Preach?" the woman's voice echoed over the receiver.

"Hey. You think I could see the kids?" he asked in a polite tone.

There was a brief silence, and he checked to see if he had been cut off.

"Preach, Tony is here right now. You know that you can see your kids. It's been a few months. How long are you in Valley Town?" she responded.

"I'll be here until Thursday," he said after calculating his stay. "But I'd really like to see them before then. I have a few things I have to get done."

"Yeah, I see. How about dropping by in an hour. Will that work?" she asked, not pushing with more questions.

"Tell Tony that I'm sorry to interrupt on such short notice," Chris said. He looked at the highway again and started to say something else but thought better of it. "Okay then. I'll see you in an hour."

"Preach?" Brit said. "Thank you for understanding about Tony, and thank you for the money that you've been sending."

"It's my job, Brit," he said.

"It's not your job, Preach. They are your kids. But thank you for loving them the way you do. I wish that you would come back to Valley Town," she said sternly.

Chris took a deep breath and let it out slowly.

"I can't, Brit. This place will suck me back in too far, and it'll be what sends me to hell," he said as he tried to compose himself and not let on about anything that was happening.

The devil you know, he thought again.

"Christopher, there are people in this town who love you. Don't let the rest of these bastards get you down," she said.

They hung up, and Chris started texting.

Hey, Hannah, how are things going?

Moments later, his phone buzzed.

I'm good. I'm about to head home from work. You doing anything later?

I have a few things that I have to take care of. I'm not sure how long it'll take.

Come over later? she asked.

He thought about it before responding, It would probably be too late.

Come over. Doesn't matter how late.

Tell you what, I'll text when I'm done. We can go from there.

A few minutes passed before she responded.

I want you to come over, please.

He looked at the roadway, then at his watch.

Okay, he texted back.

He looked up a name on his phone and dialed.

"Hey, Sandy. What's going on?"

"You're about to run face-first into an ambush," she said into the receiver.

"I have a plan, Sandy. I can't sit back and let them hurt Marcus and the girls."

"Just be smart. We are watching," she said and hung up.

He looked at his phone after the line dropped. He hit the ignition switch on his bike and made his iron horse growl. The roads were fairly clear, and he sent out one more text.

I'm headed toward the FARM.

You want me there? was the reply.

Yes, he texted back as he put his phone back in his cut.

He pulled out on the road and headed down what he had called "The Lost Highway."

What are you doing, Chris? he asked himself.

Distracting myself from reality, he answered.

The mess and the complications were already growing worse, and he was aware.

What is "home," Preach? the voice inside asked.

Where is "home"? he asked his own inner voice.

The old bridge drew closer, and his mind was a battlefield. In his mind, he was aware that he was running full throttle into chaos. Somewhere out there, the unknown enemy was hiding in the darkness, waiting on him to surface. If the enemy did not destroy him, the ghosts that were chasing him just might.

He pulled into the vast fortress of the FARM's compound, kicked down, and made his way through the front doors, walking past the pool tables, the bar, and the few people standing around. He now stood at the door of his room in the clubhouse. He opened the door and found Marla waiting. He looked at her and closed the door behind him. He needed a distraction. She would fit his immediate need. Then he would go see his kids. His priorities were shadowed by the chaos his choices were creating, and he knew that he was taking the wrong path. But Chris could not see the destructive ending through the delusions that his ghosts were creating.

Chapter 40

The Prodigal Son

The rest of the day was spent with Chris's youngest children. They were too young to really do more than spend time playing on the living room floor, but it had been great. Brit had been good enough to open up her home to him. Every moment of the time he spent playing took the stress and pressure off of his mind, even if it was only for a few short hours.

"Have you been by the ranch to see your dad?" Brit asked as Chris gathered his things to leave.

He looked up at her, knowing that he couldn't tell her more than the bare minimum.

"It's my next stop," he said as he shook Tony's hand and leaned in to kiss Brit's cheek.

"You coming back through again soon?" Tony asked as he tried to ignore the two saying goodbye.

Chris looked at them both and then looked at the little ones who now lay sleeping on a pallet.

"I'll send a check in a few weeks, Brit," he said as he reached into his cut to pull out his money roll.

He counted out several bills, folded them up, and placed them in Tony's hand.

"Take care of those babies," he said as he shook Tony's hand again more firmly, conveying a nonverbal message.

"You know I will, Preach," Tony said sincerely.

Chris looked back at Brit and the kids and opened the door to leave. He walked out to his bike and sped off into the distance. The cold wind burned his exposed skin. The weather was like a roller coaster in the northeastern Alabama mountains. A single day could bring sunshine and warmth, and the next could bring overcast clouds and cold that a man could feel deep in his bones. Today, the mountain air was ripping at his skin with bitter coldness.

So many parts of him had grown accustomed to the coldness. Since his mother had died, he had closed up into a cocoon of emotional darkness. When he'd left Valley Town, he'd walked away from his kids and his father and his younger brother and their families. He had made sure to send money every month for his kids but hadn't put any effort into reconciling with his dad.

Until today.

He turned onto Old Federal Mountain Highway and made his way into the farmlands of Valley Town. He drove to the old ranch house. He had not come back to the home of his mother and father since April three years ago. He knew that he really didn't have a choice now, though.

The men at the old farmhouse hadn't known he was there, so he had had some time to get everything ready. It would open up the door to Marcus's location. Some unknown alliance had plans to flush him out by using his family's ranch, so he would set the trap himself. He had been taught to never build fortresses to protect himself; to isolate himself would place him in worse danger. But in this situation, he would use that life lesson as a Trojan horse to lure his enemy into his own trap. He knew that if he forced them to act first, he would be in control, forcing them to abandon their strategies. That would give him the opening to play his cards. He would then be in a position to crush his enemy completely, both physically and mentally.

"Son, plan until the very end," his father had always told him.

It was the best lesson that his father had ever taught him.

He kicked down his bike in the front drive of the ranch. He looked down at his phone and back up at the driveway, then sent out a text and placed his phone back in his cut.

"Christi?" a man's voice asked.

Chris looked up and over at the front porch. It had been a long time since he had heard that name. His father had called

210

him "Christi" since birth. It was his way of expressing emotion. Deep inside, Chris welcomed it.

"Christi? Son?" his father said in an emotional tone.

Chris watched him come down the steps to him.

"Hey, Pop," he said with a half-smile.

"Christi! My God, it's really you!" the elder said as he grabbed Chris and pulled him into a hug.

He reluctantly hugged his father back.

"Pop, I need you to go to Mama Lou's place for a few days," he said coldly.

His father was lost in emotion and didn't register Chris's words.

"Christi, where have you been?" his father asked as he pulled himself back to look at his son.

"Pop, there's trouble coming this way. I need you to go to the old house," Chris said more sternly. He took his father's arm and looked directly into his eyes. "Pop. I need you to listen to me. There are some very bad people coming this way, and I can't let you be here when they come."

Lam, his dad, looked at him, and Chris knew what was coming.

"If you are in trouble, I ain't going anywhere. My son has come home. That's all that matters," he said as he started walking toward the house.

Chris watched him, then bowed his head and shook it, knowing that there would be no compromising. The two men entered the house, and his dad opened the gun cabinet next to the office door. He removed a 30/30 Winchester and several boxes of shells, followed by a double-barrel 12-gauge shotgun and shells for it.

"Load these, and I'll be right back," his dad said as he walked into the hallway leading to the bedrooms.

Chris looked at the rifle and the Old Henry 12-gauge and couldn't help but smile. The force coming to the ranch would have far more high-tech weapons than these. Just as he started to imagine an old Clint Eastwood flick, his father emerged from the bedroom wearing his twin ivory-handled .38-special revolvers that had belonged to his own father. He looked at Chris and smiled.

"Damn good to see you, boy!" he said as he pushed his way to the garage door.

Chris followed, still trying to figure out a way to get his father to abandon the idea of staying at the ranch. He stepped out into the garage, where his father was unlocking the closet door within the workspace.

"How many we thinking, Christi?" his dad asked, wheeling out a large plastic container.

"Pop, this isn't your fight. I need you to go up to the old house," Chris said again.

His dad acted as if he hadn't heard him.

Chris turned toward the window of the garage as he heard what sounded like a mixture of bikes and SUVs. His dad looked up and out, and they watched the small convoy sweep into the rear of the ranch.

"Eric...?" Chris thought out loud.

His dad looked at him and said, "I called him when you first pulled in."

"Pop—" Chris began to argue.

His dad didn't look up, but he spoke almost violently when he said, "Christi, if it's your fight, it's our fight." He opened up the container, revealing a layout of high-caliber weapons. "I don't want to hear another word about it."

Eric and three of his buddies entered the garage with their hunting rifles. Chris looked at his brother, and the two men remained silent as their father handed out weapons.

Eric leaned in to his older brother and whispered, "I am my Brother's keeper..."

Chris looked at him for a second, and they embraced.

"Always," Chris responded.

He pulled his cell from his cut and sent out a text.

"The calvary is en route," he said as he and his brother handed out full magazines to his peers.

Their dad hit the garage door button, opening it to expose a wide pasture. Just over two hundred yards away were the stables, one on the right, the other a little farther away on the left.

"Eric, you and your guys find a good spot up there. Christi and I will wait on his Brothers and set up on this side," their dad ordered.

Eric and his peers ran toward the stables, a load of weapons in tow. The small group then split up, heading in opposite directions of the stables.

"Pop, this isn't about me," Chris began.

His dad looked at him before saying, "It's about Family, Christi. Marcus and those girls are Family."

Chris turned his head toward his father but spoke not a word. He wasn't sure how his father knew about Marcus's predicament.

"We have about an hour to get ready. They have no idea that we are privy to their plan," Chris said after looking at his cell phone. "They are coming here to engage with you and flush me out."

His dad smiled at him and said, "Well, they just shook the hornet's nest."

Chris looked at his phone again as it vibrated.

I don't know what's going on, but I'm praying for you, Hannah had texted him.

Chris studied it for a second before responding with, I'm fine.

Well, I have you in my thoughts strongly, she responded.

Chris put his phone away but was puzzled by the text from Hannah.

How could she know?

The two men continued gathering gear. His dad looked up toward the old stable, where Eric had positioned himself for the clearest view of the front gate and the west gate. His friends had split up and set up positions in the front stable and along the creek bank. This covered the front gate and the east gate. Nothing would come in by surprise either by air or land.

Chris took a deep breath and continued loading the extra magazines. There was a storm brewing, and it was bringing chaos in its wind. Now it was just a waiting game. One thing had been established: Family stood by Family regardless of the circumstances. But would this be enough to bring healing? Or would it ultimately make the issues they already had worse?

Chris's cell phone buzzed, and he looked at the three texts that came in back-to-back. He looked up at his father, who was busy setting up firing positions throughout the front of the house. He had already sent his new wife to her son's home in Mentone.

Mac: Preach, we are in position, as requested.

Gabriel: Hawk in the sky.

Private number: "Be still and know that I am God." Psalm 46:10.

Chris looked at the last text again.

God, protect my Family and help me get to Marcus and the girls.

His dad walked into the room where he was working. He had a strange look on his face and was clearly pale. He handed Chris a small brown envelope. Inside of it was a little card that had a handwritten message on it. Psalm 46:10. Psalm 144:1. Psalm 91, was penned in his mother's red ink. The two men looked at the words together.

"This was on the table. We found it a couple of weeks ago but didn't know how to get it to you," his dad said.

Chris looked out at the stables and back at his father.

"Pop, I just got a text. I'm gonna ride up the road and look into a closed position," he said as he handed his father his grandfather's Winchester. "The 'Old Hawk' would want you on this weapon," he said, referring to his mother's father, John. "I'll be right back."

He headed out to his bike and dialed a number on his cell, awaiting the voice on the other side.

"I'm coming in," he said, then ended the call.

Glimpses of the day flashed into his mind. He had spent valuable time with his youngest kids, and his father and Eric had come to protect the family ranch. It was time for him to protect them all.

Plan till the end.

He smiled. He looked back at the porch, where his father stood with the old 30/30 under his arm.

"Christi!" his father yelled.

Chris looked at the elder, awaiting his next words.

"I'll see you when we get there, Christi," he said.

Chris nodded at his father and rode to the old county bridge. He would protect them in a different way: surrender.

Chapter 41

Seven

Chris kicked down on the east side of the old bridge. Nothing was on the road in either direction, and he walked to the center of the green metal structure. The ranch was fully protected, as planned. There had been a few small adjustments to handle, but it had worked out better than expected. His father's ranch would be protected on every corner if the rest of the plan fell apart. It would have been better to have watched his father drive off to the Georgia side of the mountain, but he also knew that now his family would be isolated from the impending danger.

A light drizzle of rain began to fall, making small rings in the water below. He looked out at the bend of the river and found the concrete overlook where he had stood only days before. He turned to watch the first of the scouting vehicles come into position near the bridge. Up to the right of the bridge, a black SUV stopped, and he could see the passenger's side door open. He assumed that the passenger was either viewing him and the bridge's surroundings with binoculars or the scope of a rifle. To the left of the bridge, heading up the valley's ridge line, were a dozen bikes. They resembled ancient horsemen prepared for their battle charge. Neither of the groups were friendly.

Chris watched as two of the bikes moved in toward him. They would do the initial security check and ultimately secure their prisoner. He leaned onto the rail of the bridge and lit his cigar. He kept his focus on the incoming riders, but he knew that it was the SUVs that would sweep down and take him to wherever they desired.

There were obviously other options. He could make a final stand in the middle of the old bridge. He could also make a last-ditch effort to escape via the icy waters below. But he had come to this location with a purpose: to surrender. And that's exactly what he would do.

Two riders pulled up on both sides of where he stood. Their compact semi-automatic weapons were trained on him. He walked toward them, his cigar clenched in his teeth.

"I'm unarmed," Chris said as he opened up his cut and turned around for the sentries to secure the bridge.

Another SUV made its way down the right side of the bridge, and three Russian-speaking men exited the vehicle and aggressively seized Chris, slamming him into the side of the car. One used a sophisticated wand to detect any weapons or tracking devices. The other held him forcefully against the American-made SUV. The third man stood to the right of them with a .223 assault rifle, getting secure views of the bridge and the banks of the river below. The two riders, still hidden behind their red bandanas, had positioned themselves on each end of the bridge.

Chris did not resist, regardless of his captives' aggression. After a thorough inspection, they put him in the rear of the vehicle and waited for both bikes to fall into position to escort their convoy. The other ten riders fell into position to the front and rear of the two SUVs once back on Valley Highway.

Chris kept his eyes forward and said nothing as the three Russians glared at him, watching his every move. One of the men scrolled through the current call list and text messages on his phone to see if he had contacted anyone to inform them of his current circumstances.

"Where is your other device?" the overly aggressive Russian questioned in broken English.

Chris grinned but said nothing.

"I asked you question!" the man yelled.

Chris remained silent as he watched the passenger side occupant take the phone, plug it into a laptop, and begin typing. He knew the procedure would allow them to detect all erased calls and texts, and they could disable the GPS. He silently remained aware of the situation while not resisting.

One of the bikers signaled to the SUV driver, and one of the men sitting beside Chris grabbed his leathers and pulled him closer, placing a thick black pillowcase-type covering over his head. He remained silent yet aware of the movements of the vehicle and the men inside. When they spoke, it was in Russian only, unless they were directly speaking to him. The SUV and its convoy drove another fifteen minutes before turning into a parking lot and making their way to the rear of the buildings.

"Nine hundred and twelve," Chris whispered under his breath as they pulled him from the SUV and led him into a doorway.

He could hear the sounds of machinery, possibly CNC machines being used to cut sheets of steel or rock. The covering over his head was blocking him from seeing anything or taking in the smells of the room. The two men walking to his left and right restricted his movement. He had an idea of his location but couldn't be 100 percent sure. One thing was for sure: He was about to find out.

One of the men leading him spoke to the other, and they entered a doorway that took them down a long hallway. Chris could feel the change in room temperature and was now aware that he had stepped into an office section of wherever they had led him.

"Take that ridiculous sack off of his head," a man's voice thundered as he drew closer to Chris and his guardians.

Chris's eyes took a second to adjust to the brightness of the light. He looked up and glared at the men beside him and then turned his sights toward the man talking.

"My friend, it's been a very long time, hasn't it?" the man said as the guards forced Chris into a chair inside an empty room that, by the look of all the outlets in the wall, had once been used for some type of telecommunications.

Chris looked up at the man standing over him and, without any sign of emotion, said, "Devon, our friendship died in Brownsville."

218

Devon laughed and leaned down, his hands behind his back.

"Oh my, do I sense a little bit of anger in your voice?" he asked, smirking.

"Devon, you know where we stand."

Devon walked around him, took the blade from his rear waist-line, and put it close to Chris's throat.

"And where is it exactly that we stand, Preach?" Devon asked as his facial expression changed dramatically.

Chris took a moment to think to himself before answering.

Rule number five: Remain patient and appear humble.

The faces of Mac, Marcus, and the Kid flashed through his mind. He pressed his own skin into the razor-sharp blade, bringing blood to the surface.

"We are no longer anything. The Brother that I once knew died in Brownsville, Texas, when his blade took the life of one of his own." Chris turned his eyes directly on Devon. "The day that the Butcher was born was the day that my Brothers died. So, now you can either kill me or put that blade back in its leather before I use it to gut you like a pig."

Chris wiped his throat, and Devon laughed as he stepped back from him.

"You aren't exactly in any position to make threats, my lost Brother," Devon mocked.

Chris scanned the empty room and then asked, "So, are you going to introduce me to the mysterious Señor Cruz?" standing up abruptly from his chair.

The two guards stepped backward out of surprise, and Devon stepped to the side wall, out of harm's reach. Chris grinned but said nothing. The two guards reluctantly moved toward him and took his arms on both sides. Devon slowly moved closer to him and gave his stomach a crushing blow. The pain rushed through his body, but he remained silent.

"Take him into the main office," Devon commanded.

Chris looked at the fear in one of the man's eyes.

"Don't worry, kid. I'm not here for you," he said.

The young Russian shoved him forward, ignoring his words.

"Okay then," Chris said playfully as he walked out of the room and back down the hallway.

He was led into a large office overlooking a warehouse floor. Water jet machines and CNC machines were being operated by unsuspecting employees doing their jobs. He scanned the floor, looking to find the exits on both sides of the warehouse floor.

"Sit down," the young Russian said as he pointed to an expensive leather couch.

Chris could hear mumbled chatter coming from the hallway, and the voices were getting closer to the door. The first to enter was a young biker wearing "Skully" colors, followed by two others. The fourth man was Rockhound, and he was next to Devon. Chris wanted to stand up and lunge at the two men but knew better in this situation. He had a plan, and he would follow it.

The next to enter the room were a couple of Mexican cartel soldiers. Chris knew they had all been sent ahead to secure the room before the main boss entered. And he was right. A tall, expensively dressed Mexican stepped in and looked at Chris. He never took his eyes off Chris as he made his way to the mahogany desk. Chris didn't say anything, as he assumed this would be the end of the group. However, the door opened again, and an elegantly dressed woman, followed by four female associates, entered. Chris was taken by surprise but said nothing. The woman walked over to Chris and looked at him intently. After a moment, she turned and walked over to the desk, setting her bag down.

"Señor Cruz, send a few of these men out of the room," the woman said. "I would like to have some privacy with our guest."

Señor Cruz motioned with his hand, and everyone except Devon, Rockhound, and one of the bodyguards left the room.

The woman walked over to Chris and let her hands caress his face and head before she leaned in to whisper something in his ear. As she turned back around to take off her jewelry,

Chris stood up aggressively, which led to the left side of his face meeting the razor edge of an assassin's blade. A single strain of blood dropped into his beard. The beautiful young assistant had anticipated Chris's reaction and stood ready to stop further motion forward. Chris looked at her and smiled.

"Tasha Taktarov. Does that answer your question, Preach?" the elegant woman said as she turned back to face him. "My name familiar to your ears?"

She walked over to Devon and requested his blade.

Chris remained silent as the rage inside him grew stronger.

Do NOT chase the rabbit! he screamed to himself silently.

Chapter 42

Broken

Tasha turned and walked back over to Chris, Devon's blade in her hand. The men in the room watched as she stood right in front of his chair.

"Stand up," she said as she looked down at him.

Chris did not budge, nor did he say a word.

"I said, stand up!" she yelled.

He still didn't move, only looked straight ahead.

She smiled and looked at him, then at the guards to his sides.

"Let's help our guest up," she said through her teeth, not taking her eyes off him.

The men moved on her command, taking him by the arms. He shook them both off and stood up abruptly, sending both men backward in shock. Standing right in front of the woman, Chris looked down into her dark eyes.

"That's much better," she said in a sultry tone.

She reached up and ran her fingers across his face and his lips. He could taste a salty substance on her fingertips. Without a doubt, Chris knew that taste: blood. Her left hand took hold of his leather cut, and she pulled her body closer to him, sliding the razor-sharp edge of Devon's blade underneath his base-layer shirt. The blade sliced through the clothing like a hot knife would slide though butter, exposing his chest. She ran her silky hands over his skin, never taking her eyes off of his almost-tar-colored eyes. Chris did not move. He only returned her gaze.

"Why is it that you have come to visit, Preacher?" she asked.

She looked away from his eyes and watched her own hand gently move over his chest, making its way down toward his belly button and the top of his jeans.

"They tell me that you have come to surrender yourself to us. Is there truth to these rumors?" she questioned.

He didn't respond. Without warning, the back of her left hand crashed against his face with enough force to turn his cheek to the side and leave it blood red. He remained composed as the fresh blood streamed down his chin from his lips. He offered no emotional response, nor did he speak.

"I asked you a question," she said as she traced the Unforgiven patch on his leathers with the point of the blade in her hand.

She lightly bit her lower lip and turned her attention to the other patches on display.

"What exactly is it to be a Man of Valor?" she asked in her thick Russian accent.

Chris only looked at her, and her hand met the other side of his face just as hard and just as quickly.

"Is that what you are, Preach? A man of valor?" she mocked him as blood flowed freely from both sides of his face.

Rockhound walked toward them as Señor Cruz and the others watched Tasha show off her sadistic talents.

"He sent me this text telling us he was coming to us," he said, offering Tasha the phone in his hand.

She looked at him with disgust and snapped, "I didn't ask you, now did I?"

Rockhound probably wanted to respond aggressively but chose against it.

"Tasha, you can toy with him all you please, but you're wasting valuable time," he said as he took Chris by the arm roughly.

"How dare you take my toy from me?" she joked, but she gave in to Rockhound's logic.

Chris looked at his former Brother, a hint of confusion filling his mind.

"I'm taking him to the pen," Rockhound said, leading Chris to the door.

Tasha handed Devon back his blade.

"Very well. I'll play later, I'm sure," she said, watching Chris as he was led to the office door.

The other two guards started to follow, but Rockhound motioned for them to stay.

"Señor Cruz needs you to stay with him. I'll escort Preach to the pen," he said, looking back at the others.

Chris and Rockhound left the room and made their way down the hall. Rockhound reached into his vest and handed Chris a white and black handkerchief. Chris looked at the cloth and took it from Rockhound's hand, wiping the blood from his face. He remained composed and silent. Rockhound led him through a side door and entered a barren machinery shop.

"She wants your head, Preach," Rockhound said as he led Chris through the open bay of the shop.

Chris still said nothing, just walked with Rockhound to the next doorway. They stopped just short of the door.

"What you are about to see is going to be hard. But I'm asking you to keep it together," Rockhound said as he turned and faced Chris.

The two men looked at one another intently. Chris could already feel the blood rushing through his body. Rage would be the next emotion, and left unchecked it could lead to destruction.

Keep the plan, Preach.

Rockhound looked at the doorway and then back at Chris.

"Whatever you are planning, think it through completely," he said as he took Chris's arm and opened the door.

Chris took a deep breath, anticipating what was behind the metal door. The doorway opened up into a large holding area that most likely once housed machine parts and gearing mechanisms, along with all types of shop supplies. However, now it was being used as a methamphetamine lab on one side and a Molly lab in the center. As Chris's eyes moved around and scanned the room, his heart sunk within him. Only a monster could be soulless enough to create such a spectacle. Tears formed in his eyes as the rage grew stronger within him.

224

Without any warning, he grabbed Rockhound by the throat with one hand and grabbed him under his armpit with the other, slamming him through a sheetrock wall. The two men landed with Chris positioned on top. His grip on Rockhound's throat tightened, cutting off the air and the blood from his body. Rockhound tried to struggle his way free, but the grip on his throat, along with Chris's knee pressing into his sternum, made it nearly impossible. His eyes grew wider as he tried his best to speak. Chris raised his right hand and began a series of destructive blows to the man's face, the image of what he had seen still flashing through his mind. The rage had overtaken him, and he slammed his fist into Rockhound's face again and again.

"Lo-ok be-hind you!" Rockhound finally managed to say just as one of the workers of the Molly lab hit Chris in the left shoulder with a large pipe.

Chris fell to the floor, his eyes now trying to focus on the room to his left.

"Marcus…" he mumbled as the pipe crashed against his body again. "Marcus…"

His body went limp and unconscious.

"Marcus is the least of your worries, Preach," a Russian man's voice whispered into his ear as he drifted into the darkness.

***

"Ivan, you tease him. How naughty," Tasha playfully said as she walked up beside her husband.

Ivan and his bodyguards brushed past Tasha and her assistants without acknowledging them. The women followed them, leaving Chris face down on the floor.

Two Skullys helped Rockhound to his feet and walked him into a side room to sit down. His face was swollen already, blood streaming down his face. There were multiple lacerations around his swollen eye sockets, and there was facial trauma. The dentures that were once housed in his mouth lay crushed on the floor.

Another set of men lifted Chris's lifeless body up and carried him into the room on the left, handcuffing him to the chain that was attached to the overhead crane running across the beams that were once used to lift and carry heavy machine parts to the docking area.

***

Chris woke up from a cold shock of water hitting his body. The man above him had clearly been waiting on his body to react. His wrists were both cuffed to the chain attached to the overhead crane above him, and he instinctively reacted by fighting the bonds.

The door opened, and Tasha entered.

"Leave me," she commanded the reluctant guard. "I said, leave!" she said more forcefully to the man.

She walked to where Chris was crouched on his knees. She pressed the overhead crane controls on the wall next to Chris's head and forced the chain to raise his arms up and suspend his body. The cuffs slipped on his wrist, and he grabbed ahold of the metal to stop it from ripping through his flesh. Now he stood directly in front of her, unable to do anything but stand defenseless, his arms above him. She lifted his face in her hand, forcing him to look at her.

"Ahh...the mighty one that everyone is afraid of is real," she teased.

She ran her fingers lightly from his face to his neck, tracing her fingers down his chest and torso.

"So pretty," she said as she touched and admired his bare chest, running her hand through the hair and tracing his scars.

"Why do they fear you? Tell me? No?" she played. "I have hoped for this day since the first time my husband spoke of the ghost I knew he feared."

She stepped closer, grabbing his hair and pulling it back aggressively. She kissed his neck, and her tongue danced on his chest as she verbally teased him, teasing herself at the same time. He

226

resisted and pulled his head away as much as he could. She sharply forced his head to look toward the large glass window. The pain in his body did not match the torment inside his heart and mind.

"Do you like what my puppets have done?" she questioned. "The Butcher has done well? No?"

A single tear ran down Chris's cheek. He looked at his tormentor, the anger and rage rising up stronger inside of him.

"Let them go, and I'm yours," he said as he stared into her cold eyes.

She released her grip and motioned in the air with her hand.

"My pretty man, you are already mine regardless. Now, watch your 'Family' perish," she said coldly.

Chris's fists clenched, causing the cuffs to cut into his wrists more.

In the other room, the man who once stood over Chris moved toward Marcus's bloody and naked body, which was cuffed to the wall with chains. Two female bodies lay naked and motionless on the floor in front of him. The man grabbed one of the women by the hair and forced her to stand, walking her to the window. Chris watched in horror as Ruth's battered face pressed against the window in front of him. She made eye contact with him for a moment but then collapsed to the cold floor. Her eyes clearly betrayed the face that she had been given a heavy dose of Molly, which explained their nudity. Tasha's male assistant turned his attention back to Marcus. He walked over to Marcus's naked and severely beaten body and hit him in the stomach, making him cringe from pain.

As much as Chris hated seeing the images in front of him, at least he knew that Marcus and Ruth were still alive. The second female was still unknown. All he could tell from his position was that she was a blonde. Because of this, he knew that it couldn't be Anna.

Tasha laughed as she watched Chris's reactions and the spectacle taking place on the other side of the window.

"Ivan fears a harmless shadow. A man of empty legend," she mocked.

She turned toward the door and left Chris in the room alone. The man beating Marcus stopped at Tasha's command and made his own exit from the room.

Several moments went by as Chris watched his mentor's body struggle to remain standing and conscious. Marcus looked at the women on the floor, then looked up at the window. He seemed to realize that someone was there and appeared to be straining to see who was watching him. Tears ran down Chris's cheeks, mixing into his blood-soaked beard. All at once, Marcus's face filled with realization. He was trying to speak, but Chris could not understand him.

"Ni-ne-t-een..." Marcus's lips moved slowly as he tried to form a word.

Chris tried to read his lips but couldn't make out the syllables. Marcus repeated himself a few more times before losing consciousness because of the pain and the drugs coursing through his veins.

Nineteen?

Suddenly, as if a lightning bolt had struck deep inside of him, Chris's body was full of energy. He began looking around the empty room, his eyes searching. He grabbed the chains holding him captive and swung his feet upward, slamming them into the controls of the crane on the wall. He kicked the mechanism until it lowered the chain. Once on the ground, he forced his right hand through the cuff, ripping soft tissue from his hand. He reached into his cut and retrieved a small cigar cutter and tool, then used one of the pins to unlock his left cuff. He reached into his rear pants pocket and found the black and white cloth Rockhound had given him to clean the blood from his face. The damage to his hand was superficial but painful to the touch. Blood ran freely from his face and hand. He began wrapping his hand with the cloth, and that was when he saw the red ink. In large handwriting, written in red marker, was the number twelve.

Chapter 43

The Revolution Begins

Chris opened the door slowly and checked the hallway in both directions. Empty. He immediately opened the door that led to Marcus, Ruth, and the second female. Marcus tried to look up at Chris, but his head dropped back to his chest.

"Help the girls, Preach," Marcus's struggling voice slurred.

Chris looked at the naked women and back at Marcus.

"Please, Preach," Marcus whispered.

Chris turned his attention to the women. Ruth lay on her side, too drugged to move. The other woman had her hands underneath her, and her head was facing away from Ruth and Chris. Chris looked around the room and opened a closet. He pulled a set of blankets from the shelves. He first covered Ruth and then checked her vitals. Her heart rate was slow, and her respiration was shallow, but her eyes looked steadily at him. He moved to the second woman and slowly rolled her limp body on its side, covering her with the second blanket. Her eyes were staring straight ahead. He placed his fingers on her neck to find a pulse. Nothing. He closed his eyes and took a deep breath.

"Damn it!" he cursed under his breath, then moved toward Marcus.

The leather straps buckled to Marcus's wrists were cutting off his circulation, and his hands were blue and white from the lack of blood. His face had been badly beaten, and dried blood covered several areas of his head. The stripes and ripped tissue on his chest, legs, and back painted a grotesque picture of blood and skin leaking down his naked body.

"Ruth?" he whispered.

Chris looked at his old friend and then back at the elderly woman covered in a blanket.

"Marcus, she is alive. But I need to figure out how to get you both out of here," Chris said as calmly as possible.

Marcus forced his head to face Chris and ordered, "You get my wife out of this hell."

Chris started to say something, but Marcus stopped him short.

"I'll be okay, son. Get those girls out of here," he said as he looked at his wife.

Chris looked at the door and then back at the women.

"Stephanie?" Marcus asked, referring to the second woman.

Chris looked at him and just shook his head.

Marcus closed his eyes and cried, "No..."

Chris looked at him strangely and said, "I'm sorry, Marcus. Let's get you and Ruth out of here."

He stood up to check the hallway again, and Marcus crawled over to Ruth and held her in his arms.

"Son, you can't get both of us out at the same time," he said as he kissed her head.

"Marcus, I'm not leaving this room without you," Chris said.

Marcus mustered up enough strength to forcefully use his voice to say, "You listen to me, boy! This is my queen. You protect your queen! I'm not asking. I'm telling you. Get my queen to safety."

Chris walked over to kneel beside Stephanie's body. He reached down and closed her eyes. Marcus was rocking Ruth in his arms, tears running down his face.

"Baby, you have my heart. I have loved you the best I can," he whispered into her ear.

Chris looked down at them and gently said, "Marcus, we have to move now."

He then reached down and picked Ruth's body up in his arms.

Marcus stood and struggled to lean against the wall, then said, "Son, promise me that you will protect my queen."

Chris studied the situation and said, "I'll be right back," as he started out the door.

"Promise me!" Marcus said strongly.

Chris looked down at Ruth and back at Marcus and answered, "I give you my word, Brother."

Marcus acknowledged him with a grin. The pain was ripping through his body. Chris could see it in his eyes.

"I'll be right back," he said as he and Ruth slipped out and headed to the door at the end of the hallway.

He opened the door and looked out into an empty parking lot.

"Okay, here we go," he whispered.

He held Ruth tightly and began running as fast as he could to the tree line on the other side of the pavement.

"Stop!" commanded a man's voice.

Chris looked in his direction and saw the assault weapon being aimed to fire. He looked down at his cargo and then back up at the tree line again.

"Ruthy, this is gonna sting a little," he said as he pushed off into a sprint again, diving into the thorn bushes and overgrown brush.

He landed in a position that guarded Ruth from the impact the best he could. Quickly, he secured her and moved to his right to maneuver his way out of the gunman's line of fire and separate himself from her body. The gunman stood at the edge of the thicket, searching for his prey. Chris continued moving deeper into the trees, making as much noise as possible to lure his predator. A few hundred feet into the darkness of the trees, he found an old creek bed that was possibly a drainage ditch from one of the buildings behind him. He scanned the bed of the creek, looking for something he could use as a temporary weapon.

Force the enemy into the rabbit hole.

He could now hear two, possibly three, assailants moving into the trees. He peeked over the moss and saw the first gunman moving slowly in his direction, diligently searching the brush with his eyes.

"Gotcha," Chris whispered, lying down in the creek ditch

The man passed by him, and his face was full of both shock and fear when Chris grabbed his legs and ripped them from the earth's foundation. His face and body smashed into the ground. Chris sprung on top of the man, securing his weapon and slamming it aggressively into the back of the man's head, leaving him unconscious. Chris immediately ripped the man's belt from his pants and secured his arms, one to the front and the second to the rear, the belt running between the man's legs, leaving him no way to escape.

The second man was less than twenty yards away but couldn't see Chris through the high brush between him and the creek bed. Chris checked the weapon, unlocked the safety, and set the weapon to semi-automatic. He crouched on his knees and searched for the third assailant.

"Come on, boy. Let's play," Chris said.

A noise behind the man took him by surprise. He turned to react, but it was too late. The man's chest burst open, and his eyes turned wild and confused. Ten seconds later, Chris heard the echo of a high-powered rifle sounding off in the distance.

"One click..." Chris calculated.

The man's body dropped into the creek, and a third assailant rushed straight into the second shot, his left leg separating from his body. Immediately, the man's panic set in, and he began screaming in Russian.

Gabriel.

The man looked up to see Chris standing above him.

"You're going to die," the man said, looking up at his prey.

Chris looked at the man. Rage and anger tried to control him.

"I'll see you in hell, then," he said with a smile.

He reached down and took the man's weapon, then used his boot to kick the man into the murky and stagnant water below.

There was only one direction that shot could have come from: somewhere across the pavement that separated the trees and the warehouses. Chris moved slowly back to where he had left Ruth. He knew that Gabriel, or whoever made those shots, had him covered from above. Ruth was alert and was trying to remain calm in her hiding place.

"Ruth, I have to go back inside," he said as she looked up at him.

She couldn't speak but patted his hand.

Chris handed her the second weapon and asked, "Do you know how to work this?"

When she shook her head no, he gave her a quick lesson.

"Point and fire," he said, smiling.

She nodded.

"Okay then. I'll see you in a minute," he said.

He checked the parking lot and ran back to the door he had exited with Ruth. Two SUVs rushed toward him, firing rounds that danced around him. He stopped and took a knee, firing at the closest vehicle. The rounds from his weapon hit the SUV's engine and front tires, causing the driver to lose control, and the speed sent metal and rubber spinning in the air. The vehicle crashed onto the black pavement.

He immediately turned his attention to the secondary vehicle, but before he could do anything, three motorcycles came from behind the SUV. He aimed at them but stopped when he saw that the bikers were throwing grenades at the second SUV. He took to his feet and raced toward a trash bin, seeking shelter. He could hear the engines of the Harleys racing by his position just as the SUV exploded into the concrete ramp of the building, which was adjacent to where he was located. He looked across to where he had left Ruth. A dozen fully equipped men surfaced from the tree line, stopped, and all dropped to their knees in the brush between the pavement and his own location.

"Travis?" he asked as he saw his old friend leading the group.

Chris raised his right fist into the air. Travis and the other eleven men followed suit. Then Travis signaled for the others to stay in their position and raced over to Chris's hiding place.

"Hey, Brother," Travis joked.

Though Chris was happy to see him, he wasn't amused. Chris looked over at Ruth's position.

"We got her, Preach," Travis confirmed.

Chris looked at him, and they both moved in unison toward the door. The element of surprise was gone. They could hear weapons being fired from the front of the building. The roar of motorcycles echoed in the night sky. The sound of high-caliber rounds followed from time to time. Travis set his team into motion, and five of them moved Ruth to safety. The other six formed a perimeter to cover all exits. Travis pulled a set of Karambit blades from his belt and handed them to Chris. Chris smiled.

The two men moved to the door and made their way to where Chris had left Marcus. The room was empty. Chris looked at the wall. A trail of blood ran out into the hall and went all the way to the other end. They slowly made their way down the empty hall and opened the door leading into the warehouse full of unused machines.

"You take the right, and I'll go left," Travis whispered.

Chris agreed and moved to his side. They moved forward on both sides. Chris followed the blood trail up the center of the room with his eyes. Whoever had Marcus was forcing him to move in that direction.

The old man still has fight in him.

Travis turned at the end of his wall, and Chris met him in the middle. Chris put his back to the wall and took a deep breath. Travis studied him.

"You can't do this solo, Preach," he said.

Chris looked at him and started to respond, but Travis spoke first.

"I know you. We will move through this next door, and you will move alone to find Marcus," Travis said.

"I'm aware of the 'team' effort, Trav. There's too much at stake for me to go maverick," Chris assured his friend.

Travis looked at the door and back at Chris.

"Okay. You take the lead. I have your six," Chris said as he started to open the door.

Weapons of several calibers sounded off in the near distance. Chris took a kneeling position at the open doorway, and Travis moved forward. Chris followed three or four feet behind Travis's lead.

"Preach, watch—" a voice screamed, trying to warn the two men.

It was too late. The first cut carved its way through Chris's leather like a hot knife through butter. The pain was masked by the adrenaline and shock running through him. Chris used his rifle to block the fast-moving hands of his attacker, but one of the blades sliced his arm, forcing him to drop the weapon. He saw Travis move into position to fire his weapon, but shots were fired, missing him by inches. Chris scrambled to regain position and avoid the blades and watched as Travis found cover and returned fire in the general direction of the incoming fire.

"Preach, I've waited a very long time for this day," the man said as he waved his blades in Chris's direction.

Chris searched for Travis and found him dealing with his own issues. He then saw his own weapon lying on the floor behind his foe.

"Devon. Why?" Chris asked.

Devon laughed and moved closer. It was almost like a dance between the two men.

"Money," Devon responded.

Chris looked at him, watching his hands, and said, "You butchered the Kid. He had a family. A life."

Chris pressed the quick release on both of the Karambits and held them out. Devon moved in quickly and tried to make another slice on Chris's flesh. He aimed at his right arm, then used the other blade to search out Chris's left neck artery. Chris maneuvered away from him. The firefight to Chris's right had stopped. There was no sound coming from Travis's position. Devon smiled as he realized Chris's dilemma.

"They all fall sooner or later," he teased.

Chris returned the smile, and Devon changed direction and moved in again on Chris.

"The Butcher. That's what the Lost Boys have called me since Brownsville," Devon said, continuing to toy with Chris's emotions.

Chris remained calm, watching his assailant. Devon moved forward and overreached, allowing Chris to spin to his left and attack. One of his Karambits sliced into Devon's right bicep, and the second blade sliced horizontally up Devon's chest and throat. Chris turned quickly in the opposite direction, sending Devon through a plate-glass window. When he landed, Devon lay with his eyes wide open. Chris looked down at Devon's lifeless body, then back looked back toward Travis's position.

Blood ran down Chris's arm and chest. The ruined remains of cloth under his leather hung like tassels. He picked up his rifle and made his way to Travis. He turned the corner and found Travis crouched beside a man sitting on the floor near the far wall. Chris made his way to the two men. Travis looked up at Chris, and Chris looked around Travis to see the face of the lifeless man.

"Rockhound!" Chris said in confusion and disbelief.

"He tried to warn us," Travis said as he took the 9 mm from his grip.

Chris looked around the warehouse full of machines.

"What is happening, Trav? This doesn't make sense," he said.

Travis looked down at Rockhound's body again and said, "I don't know, Preach."

Chris walked toward the office windows. Three men lay dead inside.

"This is too easy," Chris whispered. He turned and looked at Travis. "What is this all about, Travis? This can't be because I came back."

Travis looked at his phone, then back up at Chris, and answered, "You coming back has just opened the gates."

"What the hell does that mean?" Chris asked.

Travis walked over to Chris and put his hand on his shoulder.

"I don't know, Preach. But I can tell you this: Your return caused the snakes to come out of their holes," he said.

Chris thought about it.

"Vladimir, Ivan, Cruz..." he listed out loud.

Travis opened the door. Silence was all they heard now. The firefight outside had ended.

"But..." Chris started to question.

Travis turned to listen, and Chris didn't finish his thought out loud.

"We need to find Marcus," he said and turned to look back at the bodies lying on the concrete floor. "I want Rockhound's body taken to the FARM."

Travis nodded in affirmation.

"There are drums of diesel out back. Burn the rest," Chris said as he walked out the door.

Outside, there were a couple dozen Lost Boys and another dozen mercs. Ruth sat with a large group of women from fifteen to fifty years old. The Russians had been using most of them for years in their sex trade and slavery operations.

"I'm far from perfect, but this has to end," Chris said as they walked toward the crowd.

He looked at Ruth and headed in her direction.

"Marcus?" she asked as she looked up at him.

Chris looked at her and the rest of the women.

"I'll find him, Ruth. I give you my word. I will find him."

"Get these Sisters home," Travis ordered one of his men.

A large black SUV pulled up, and the passenger door opened. Sandy stepped out and looked at Chris. Gabriel exited the right-side rear door carrying his .223 long rifle. Chris smiled at his son, and Gabriel gave him a subtle gesture.

"Come with me," Sandy said as Chris moved closer to the SUV.

Chapter 44

Choices

Sandy looked at Chris, and without a word spoken, there was complete understanding. Chris was going in alone.

He motioned for one of the men sitting on a Harley to come to where the SUV idled. Chris and Gabriel opened up the covered trailer, and Chris stepped in to find his motorcycle waiting. Gabriel just smiled at his father, seeming to know that he had made his old man happy. From within the trailer, Chris hit the ignition switch, making the beast roar. He backed his bike out, and Sandy tossed Gabriel Chris's helmet. Travis pulled out a cigar and handed it to Chris. Smiling, Chris lit the edges of the high-dollar tobacco. Smoke circled from his lips.

"I'll be right back," Chris said, smiling at his son.

Sandy signaled for him to pull alongside her.

"Ro is out there somewhere, Chris," she said, looking at the blood drying on Chris's chest.

Chris took her shoulder and said, "I got this, Sandy," trying to encourage her.

She looked at Travis and Gabriel, then looked back at Chris.

"I don't know how deep this goes, but don't trust anyone," Sandy whispered into his ear.

Chris felt like the world was closing in on him from all sides. He hadn't come back to Valley Town to get pulled into a web this deep. But now he was locked in a position that he couldn't walk away from. He had people he loved involved. Marcus was out there injured, and people were dead. The reality was that there would be more to follow.

Chris looked at the group around him. Gabriel was a good kid. He didn't want to drag him into this any further. While he and Sandy had been friends for twenty-plus years, he wasn't sure about her motives.

Then there was Hannah. She had become a major part of his thoughts. He knew that he had to sabotage that as soon as possible. She was better than the life he could offer her. It was just a matter of time before she realized that herself and left him like everyone else did. It would be safer for him to do the damage himself. It would hurt less. It was like ripping a Band-Aid from skin, slow was painful. The faster, the better.

Right now, the situation required him to react. That reaction was going to come with consequences. The seeds that had been sewn would reap a crop that he wasn't ready to harvest.

His thoughts were interrupted by Sandy's voice as she said, "Preach, it's time to move."

She held a voice-monitor wire in her hand that was designed to go underneath clothing.

Chris looked at the wire and back at Sandy.

"You have lost your damn mind. I'm not wearing a wire," he said as he secured the clasp of his helmet.

"We need to record whatever goes on so we can use—"

"There won't be a need for recording," Chris interrupted.

Sandy looked at him, knowing what he was implying.

"What if you fail, Preach?" she asked.

Chris looked over at Gabriel and out at the men waiting for their next set of orders. He opened up his saddlebag and removed a small bottle of whiskey. He took a shot from the brownish-gold liquid, sealed the top, and tossed the bottle to Travis.

"If I fail, it won't matter. Remember me when you drink Jameson," he said, smiling.

Sandy looked at Travis, who was holding the bottle in his hand. Travis took a shot and tossed it to Gabriel.

Chris placed his right fist on his chest and then raised it into the air.

"Strength and honor!" he shouted.

The men waiting followed suit and, in unison, repeated his battle cry.

"Strength and honor!" they erupted.

Chris took one last look at his son. Gabriel nodded.

Chris winked at his oldest son and said, "I'll be right back," as he twisted the throttle and sped off.

***

Sandy looked at the men standing by.

"Well, let's move and set up the next position," she ordered.

Travis walked over to Gabriel and put his hand on the young man's shoulder. The two made eye contact, but nothing was said verbally.

"Take Bravo team and secure them at the FARM. Rocky is waiting on you to arrive," Travis told one of the riders.

Travis and Sandy settled themselves in the SUV and rode off, the other SUVs following.

Gabriel sent a joint text to Beau, Mac, and Sammy.

Ghost on the move.

A few seconds later, the replies came in.

Delta en route.

Echo positioned.

Mac: I have eyes on Charlie.

Gabriel and the other bikers roared off in the opposite direction of the others.

Chapter 45

Darkness Falls

The sun was beginning to drop behind the trees as Chris made his way down Old Eleven Highway. Everything was changing, and it was growing more and more intense. His body ached, and although the cuts on his arms and chest had coagulated, he could still feel the sting from the wind and turbulence as he made his way through the pines.

Images of his mother ran through his mind. After all, that's why he had returned to Valley Town.

Come Home.

He thought about the little brown paper with red ink.

I'm back, Mama. Now what?

In his mind, he could see her up the road, waving at him, her big, bright smile captivating everything around her.

Mama, I need to know what to do.

He could almost hear her whisper in his ears.

"The bell hasn't rung yet," she said, her voice echoing in his spirit.

As he sped up the old highway, the turns became sharper and sharper, like knives of a butcher's blade. The straightaway was just up ahead, and then there was the bridge separating counties. In the distance, he saw four bikes stationed on the opposite side of the bridge. As his wheels hit the edge of the bridge, it was as if the world was moving in slow motion. His brain continued at a normal pace, but he could see every detail of the riders up ahead. It was too late to react defensively to what his gut had been warning him about. He moved ahead as if not aware of the pending danger. Two riders pulled to his left, two to his right. They acted like ghost riders leading him to a safe area, but Chris knew better. Their faces were hidden, and none offered Brotherhood gestures of the Lost Boys. He would have to ride this one out.

Rule number one: Never ride solo.

He couldn't count how many times he had broken this rule. Chris was a maverick. He didn't like to rely on anyone but himself. That way, if something went wrong, no one was to blame but himself.

He smiled as if knowing a secret no one else was aware of. The riders led him to The Belle and the FARM. This time, there was no welcoming committee. No sentries welcomed him in. The gates opened, and the five riders rode through the high steel fence topped with barbed wire. The courtyard was empty as they moved beyond the walls of The Belle. Chris kicked down and slowly removed his helmet, but he kept on his gloves.

"There's my old friend," the voice behind him teased.

Chris turned his head and watched JT exit the side door of The Belle, followed by several others. The ghost riders fell in behind him, blocking an easy exit. Chris smiled as he lit his cigar and looked sideways at the active President of the Lost Boys.

"Now, who would have guessed," Chris joked as he blew out smoke.

JT walked to where Chris sat side-saddle on his bike, his gloved hands crossed left over right in his lap.

"Why didn't you just stay gone, Preach?" JT asked as he stepped in front of him. "We were doing just fine without you here."

Chris remained silent, knowing that nothing he said would really matter.

JT looked at Chris and then motioned in the air, signaling one of his Brothers to move into action. The biker knocked on the door of the clubhouse, and the door opened. JT watched Chris's reaction as he watched Marcus being shoved out of the door, followed by Anna, with Ricky Saunders bringing up the rear.

"Wayne, put my guest on their knees," JT ordered the lead biker.

Chris didn't move or show any emotion. The large red-headed man kicked Marcus in the knee, sending him to the ground, and

242

then grabbed Anna by her hair, pulling her close to him. Anna's eyes were full of tears.

Chris watched Ricky. His father had just been killed. Did he know yet? Would it matter?

The courtyard of the Lost Boys was now full of Red Skull patches, along with the white and black colors of his own club. Four black SUVs were parked in the center.

JT's face spoke a thousand words as he asked, "Tell me again, what brought you back?"

Chris puffed his cigar slowly and said, "I came back for the entertainment."

The door of the clubhouse opened up again. This time, Señor Cruz, Ivan, and Tasha exited. Señor Cruz's entourage of body-guards and a smaller set of bald ex-military-looking Russians followed Ivan and Tasha.

JT smiled as he noticed Chris bite down on his cigar.

Tasha pushed her way by her husband and stood next to JT, whispering, "Kill him now, baby," while smiling at Chris.

JT looked at the tall Russian woman and grinned.

"My pleasure," he replied.

He motioned with his right hand, and Chris readied himself to fight. Wayne pulled a weapon from his waistband and fired three shots, hitting his targets dead-on. The other bikers drew their weapons and aimed at their target. Chris watched as Ivan dropped to his knees and fell face-first onto the pavement. Ivan's bodyguards didn't have time to respond. The Skullys had them pinned down, unable to move.

Tasha stepped in closer to Chris and hissed, "I am the queen!" She looked at the bodyguards hovering over her dead husband. "Stand down."

The men relaxed and filed in behind Cruz and his group.

JT turned his attention back to Marcus and Anna. It wasn't in him to be aggressive. At his core, he was a coward who had used the science of manipulation to get where he was in the club. He knew that he had Chris in a bad position, but he also knew that Chris was not ignorant about his weaknesses.

Anna sobbed as Wayne stood over her like a dragon looming over its prey. Marcus struggled to stay upright.

Chris looked around the courtyard. "Home" was no longer home. He looked at Tasha and took a long puff from his cigar, his posture never changing.

Ricky now stood behind Señor Cruz and Wayne. Marcus and Anna remained kneeling. Chris and Marcus made eye contact, and Chris tapped his left index finger on his cut and then covered his right hand, flashing five fingers. Marcus understood the signals and nodded in affirmation. Ricky seemed to be reading Chris's strategy, as well, and moved closer to Wayne and Anna.

Chris tried to read the expressions of the young Skully. One slight move of aggression would send Chris into the offensive.

Too much emotion. Stay calm. Collect your thoughts.

He watched Ricky move just to the side of Wayne.

What are you doing, kid? he thought as he watched Ricky.

Marcus reached down and took Anna by her right hand. Chris assumed that it was to try and console her. Tasha's eyes followed Chris's, and he realized that he had betrayed himself because of his concern for Anna and Marcus. Tasha's open hand crashed across Chris's face, turning it blood red. Chris didn't show emotion this time. He simply looked at the Russian.

"If you touch him again, I'll kill you, bitch," Anna said as she looked up through her tears at Tasha. Her once-soft voice now had an aggressive tone to it.

The announcement shocked Chris as much as it did Marcus and the others.

"Did you say something, little girl?" Tasha asked as she looked at Anna.

Wayne's grip grew tighter on Anna's neck and long hair. She looked up at Wayne and then back at Tasha.

"I swear on my family's name that if you touch Preach again, it will be the last thing you ever do," Anna said bravely.

Chris looked at Marcus and then looked back at Anna.

Tasha slapped Chris's other cheek sharply, adding to the blood on his lips.

Anna looked down at the dirt for a second, then returned her gaze to Chris.

"I know who you are, Preach. My mama and daddy loved you," she said.

Chris sat up straighter in his saddle.

"My grandmother once told me stories about you and my daddy," she added.

Tasha began laughing and said, "How touching…"

Anna never took her focus off of Chris.

"I thought that you were a fictional character like Sinterklaas," she continued.

Chris smiled, fighting back emotions of his own.

Anna looked back at Tasha and JT. Wayne started to tighten his grip again, but she didn't react this time. She looked over at Marcus and whispered, "Thank you."

The first shot hit one of the bikers behind Chris, and the rest moved to seek cover. Wayne didn't have a chance. Ricky's firearm fired a single round into the large man's forehead. A second high-powered rifle shot hit just left of Chris, giving him time to respond to JT, who had just pulled his .38 from his pants. Señor Cruz and his henchmen quickly found safety in the SUVs parked in the courtyard. Ivan and Tasha's bodyguards moved into position to form a defensive, but they were met with heavy fire that pinned them behind the courtyard steps.

Rick blocked the way for Anna as she pounced on Tasha. An assassin's blade sliced its way across Tasha's face. Her hands reached up to protect her vanity. It was no use. Anna's blade sliced her face, then both wrists, and then sliced through her throat.

Chris tackled JT to the ground. The .38 fell out of his reach. One of the Skullys kicked Chris in the ribs, forcing him off of JT, which gave the president a chance to recover.

Señor Cruz's men opened the gate and made their exit. Shots fired immediately into the roof and hood of the lead SUV, stopping it in its tracks.

Chris fought against three of the young Skullys. They were getting the best of him as they hit one after the other. JT scrambled and disappeared out of sight.

Motorcycles and Jeeps roared into the FARM's courtyard from what seemed like all sides.

A solid right fist crashed against Chris's jaw, dropping him to a knee. Just as he began to move again, he saw a large, muscular man ram into one of the Skullys.

"Mac!" Chris yelled.

Mac grabbed Chris and shoved him over the line of bikes. Machine-gun fire hit the spot they had just been standing in.

Chris looked up to see the impossible: Beau, Sammy, Mac, and Travis had set up a small wall and were firing back at the SUVs. Cruz's men were relentless. The elder Lost Boys fought side by side, pushing back the Russians and the Mexican forces.

"Where's Anna!" Chris yelled.

Travis pointed toward the side of the building. Anna was safe. Rick sat with his head down, and Anna was frantically trying to help him. Chris knew he couldn't help her from his position.

Travis looked back at Anna and yelled, "Sandy! Get Marcus and the girl out of here!"

Chris watched as a Jeep sped to where Anna sat with Ricky and Marcus. Rocky was behind the wheel, and Sandy jumped out to give aid to Anna and Ricky.

Chris looked for JT and scrambled toward the clubhouse door. The room was empty, the TVs blaring sports programs. He removed both of his blades from their sheaths. His index fingers fit securely in the rings of the Karambit blades. He made his way to the sleeping quarters. The firefight outside was still going on, but the darkness had fallen like a blanket of heavy rain on Chris. The place that was once a sanctuary was now a den of vipers. JT

246

lurked somewhere within the shadows, and Chris made his way down the hall. Alone.

Never ride solo. Why do you keep breaking that rule?

He hit the light switch on the wall, but nothing happened. The breaker had been flipped. The electricity was shut down, leaving the rooms and the hallway pitch-black. There was a silence that was almost deafening as he made his way down the hallway. His imagination and his memories crashed together, and it was like a floodgate being opened, the dry banks of a riverbed being transformed instantly. The darkness compelled him to move with caution, but his flooded mind was being overwhelmed with thoughts. The hopeful fragments of light were gone, and only darkness remained.

"'Rage, rage! Against the dying of the light!'" he whispered, quoting Kim Ambrose, a scholar and teacher from his past.

Rage… Rage…

Slowly, his eyes seemed to adjust to the darkness, and he was able to make sense of the shadows. Somewhere in the darkness, his heart began opening up to visions of paradise.

What have you been fighting for, Christopher? What are you trying to accomplish? Is any of this worth the cost? The sweet voice of his mother's words echoed within his spirit.

Although she was gone from this world, right here, right now, at this moment in the darkness, she was right in front of him. Her smile radiated within the walls of this pit of vipers. The reality of his situation—the truth that remained—opened up his mind.

What are you running from?

Chris thought about the words rushing through him.

Darkness, Mama. I can't handle the darkness.

The thoughts caused him to be distracted by his surroundings. The danger lurking somewhere was real, yet he had left reality and entered a much more dangerous place: the world of his fears.

I'm alone.

He remembered that night in Murphy. The hard, cold rain that beat down on the pavement. The smell of the bar. The taste of the Irish whiskey on his lips. The smell of cheap perfume mixed with the sweat of the men trying to win the attention of women too drunk to care what circumstances and consequences would follow in the morning light.

They are lost, son, the still, small voice of his Heavenly Father, mixed with the sound of his mother's voice, echoed in his mind.

Come Home.

The memory of the note left behind once again reminded him of why he had returned.

"This is not what I came back to accomplish," he argued.

I didn't want to return to this. It's why I left, he thought.

"Before I formed thee in the belly I knew thee…" the voice said.

Chris tried to focus on the doors to both sides of the hall. Somewhere in the darkness, the enemy hid, waiting to catch his prey unaware.

"…and before thou camest forth out of the womb I sanctified thee…" the voice said.

The shadows seemed to move all around him, as if light were breaking through the pitch-blackness of his surroundings.

"…and I ordained thee a prophet unto the nations," the voice continued.

Chris began to feel the anger and hurt build up inside of him as the words of Scripture raced inside his thoughts.

"NO!" he screamed out loud.

Now mocking voices raced through his imagination and thoughts, going against his knowledge and wisdom.

You need to be more focused on the enemy within these walls than these ridiculous words, the mocking voices teased.

The hall seemed to never end as he slowly made his way to where the bathroom and showers were at the very end.

There is no escape, Preach. You have gone too far to go back now. God doesn't care about you and your memories. The mess that you have made—the lies, the bloodshed. The blood's too thick on your hands to ever wash away. You belong to me! the mocking voices taunted him.

Chris stopped and pressed his back to the wall on his left, his blades secured tightly in his fist.

That's right... Just end the pain, the evil inside him said. Cut your wrist. Slash your own throat.

Chris fought his thoughts.

End this! the voices screamed.

"Rage, rage! Against the dying of the light," a peaceful voice whispered in his mind. "Be not afraid of their faces: for I am with thee to deliver thee..."

"I can't..." Chris whispered.

Suddenly, Chris felt hands tear into his shoulder's flesh, spinning him to his right. He was still unable to see completely, but he knew that JT was attacking. He reacted out of instinct, blocking the hard fist forming in the shadows. He caught JT's arm and turned sharply to his left, then felt JT's weight leave the foundation of the floor as the two men crashed to the floor in a scramble. A second set of hands grabbed at the leather on his back. Chris was fully aware of JT's presence, but who was the second force attacking him? He scrambled to get to his feet and away from JT's grasp, and he simultaneously tried to keep the other set of talons from ripping at him.

It was too dark for them to fire a weapon. It would put both parties at risk.

His Karambits turned and twisted as he tried to slice anything moving toward him. He moved backward toward the doorway at the end of the hall. He had chased the rabbit, but the vipers had set their trap. Pain raced through his hip, the numbness spreading up his spine. The blade that was once secure in his right hand dropped to the floor somewhere beneath him.

FIGHT, CHRIS!

Chris caught the attack coming at him. He worked his way in a circle, trying to get his back off the wall. The throat of one of his attackers found itself firmly within the grip of his right hand.

He used his left hand to slice upward and his right to cut the arm attached to his now-struggling foe. A second sting hit him just above his left shoulder, next to his neck. Numbness flowed more intensely throughout his body.

That bell hasn't rung yet! Fight! he heard the voice of his spirit scream.

As the battle continued, images of Anna, Marcus, and Ricky Saunders raced through his mind, the darkness rampaging like a juggernaut.

"Christopher, let him go!" Marcus's voice said, interrupting Chris's blind rage. "Christopher! Let him go!" the voice said more intensely.

Chris looked to his right and saw Marcus and Travis standing in the once-pitch-black hallway, their lanterns illuminating the hall. He looked to his left. JT now lay face down, one of the Alpha team members securing his wrist behind his back. He turned his attention to the man in his grip.

"Will!" Chris exclaimed. Rage, anger, and confusion battled for control. "Will!" he screamed louder as he squeezed tighter.

The blade in his left hand was now pressing into Will Stone's throat. One flick of the wrist, and the blade would end the life of Chris's lifelong friend.

"Christopher, let him go. We have officers outside ready to take him and the others into custody," Travis said as he slowly moved toward Chris.

"Why, Will?" Chris asked.

"We have been trying to solve the murder of Matthew King for months. Sandy got too close to finding out Will was involved," Travis said.

Chris looked at Will and then back at Travis and Marcus.

"You killed Matty?" Chris asked in anger.

"Christopher. Please let Will go. It's time to end the bloodshed in Valley Town," Marcus begged.

"I don't understand," Chris said as he released his grip and pulled the blade from Will's throat.

Travis stepped in and spun Will to face the wall, then zip-tied Will's wrists.

Marcus grabbed Chris and moved to the front of the clubhouse. Chris struggled to scan the room. Robby, Cowboy, Bear, Gator, and several others were positioned on their knees, their hands bound behind them, lined up on the clubhouse floor next to the bar. Dead and wounded Lost Boys and Skullys lay scattered about the room. Cruz and his men had escaped. The Russian mercenaries had died because of senseless power and greed.

"I don't understand," Chris repeated.

Beau and Gabriel moved in to help Marcus with Chris. He dropped his weapon and suddenly fell to both knees. Sandy, Gabriel, and Travis moved in to assist him. Chris looked at the cut across his forearm.

"Toxins…" he said just as he lost control of his body, collapsing face-first on the pavement.

Dr. Collins ran to where he lay face down. The others frantically tried to aid him.

"Turn him over!" Dr Collins yelled. "I have to get the antidote in his bloodstream before the venom affects his central nervous system."

"Hannah…" Chris said as he drifted into unconsciousness.

Chapter 46

Rain

Hannah looked up from her Bible as the screen of her cell phone lit up the dark kitchen, which was connected to her living quarters. She walked over and looked at the number on the screen. Not recognizing the number, she turned around to walk away, but something made her look back.

"Hello?" she said, answering the call after the unknown number called again.

There was silence on the line.

"Hello? Is anyone there?"

The other person hung up, and she focused on the screen. She called the number back, and it went straight to voicemail.

She sat back down on the sofa and picked up her Bible.

"Where are you, Chris?" she pondered as her thoughts went to the man she had begun falling for.

She opened her Bible and looked at the Scripture highlighted on the page.

"First Corinthians, chapter thirteen," she read to herself.

She looked at the words on the page.

"Lord, what do you want me to do? I'm falling in love with a man I hardly know," she prayed, closing her eyes.

A single tear fell from her right eye and dropped onto the page. She looked down and saw her tear running down the page.

"'Love is patient, love is kind… It always protects, always trusts, always hopes, always perseveres,'" she read out loud. "'Love never fails…'"

She closed her eyes, and Chris's face smiling at her as he pulled into her driveway came into her thoughts.

"Father, help me love him," she prayed. "If it is your will, Lord, let me show him what love really is."

She sat in the silence of her living room, holding her Bible to her chest, her eyes still closed as she listened for God to speak to her spirit. She turned the pages of her Bible and found the Scriptures.

"'Ask the Lord for rain in the springtime...'"

She closed her eyes and opened them again, looking out her kitchen window at the rain pouring down on her patio.

"'...I will restore them because I have compassion on them. They shall be as though I had not rejected them, for I am the Lord their God and I will answer them,'" she read, but she didn't quite understand.

Hannah, he is my mighty warrior. I called him to me long ago. I will bring him back. I will show him love, the voice inside her gently whispered. Read the words I gave Paul in verse eight again.

She flipped the pages back to Corinthians.

"'Love never fails...'" she read. If you love him, love him as I love him.

She closed her Bible and stared out at the lightning strikes in the sky. Thunder crashed in the distance. The atmosphere was chaos as the hot and cold air clashed together. Rain poured down outside, creating a river in the street gutters.

God is washing the mess away.

Her cell phone rang again, startling her. She walked over and once again saw the same unknown number.

"Hello?" she said into the receiver.

There was silence.

"Hello? Is anyone there?" she said.

She could hear something on the other end of the line.

***

"I need y-you..." Chris said, straining into the cell phone.

The drugs inside him were poisoning his blood, but somehow he forced himself to call her, fighting the urge to give in and end the fight. He had to see her, so he slipped away from his Brothers at the FARM. Rockhound and several Skullys were dead. Sal, Grim, and his Brother Leadbelly from the Lost Boys were dead, as well. But at this moment, he just wanted to be close to Hannah.

***

"Chris?" she said as her entire body awakened at the sound of his voice. "Baby? Where are you?"

She grabbed her keys, not knowing where she was heading.

"Home…" he said, his voice breaking up on the line.

Hannah couldn't understand what he was saying, but she knew that he was trying to tell her something. She opened the door to her garage and got in her car. She opened the garage door and pulled out into the hard rain. She looked down the street. Lightning struck, illuminating the sky, followed by a breathtaking crash of thunder. A dark figure stumbling in the rain caught her attention.

"Chris!" she said out loud as she looked out into the darkness, the rain pouring down on the street, the solitary figure struggling to move in her direction.

She got out of her car and ran to the wounded figure. As she got closer, she realized that it was indeed Chris struggling to make his way to her. He dropped to his knees, seeming to be exhausted as he bled out on the pavement. She grabbed him, pulling him to her.

"Baby? What happened?" she asked in concern while trying to assess his injuries.

"Home…" he whispered, going in and out of coherency.

She struggled to help him up and led him to her house, the rain drenching them head to toe. His weight was almost too much for her as she struggled to hold him steady and open the door, leading them out of the rain. She helped him inside and up the stairs to her bedroom.

Chris's body was still covered with blood. His clothes were soaked with rain. His chest was exposed, and his leathers were ruined. Some type of blade had sliced through his cut, leaving

254

lacerations across his chest, his arms, and his shoulders. She looked at the blood on her own hands and then back down at Chris's body. He looked exhausted.

"God? What have I gotten myself into?" she questioned.

She peeled off his drenched clothes and the leather remains of his club colors and laid them in the corner. He tried to regain his posture, but his movement was limited.

"Chris? I need to get you to the hospital. You're hurt," she said, trying not to panic.

He opened his eyes and looked at her intently, then said softly, "Help me to the shower, Hannah."

She helped him up and to the shower. He stripped off his pants and tossed them to the side. The water from the shower ran over his naked body, the mud and the blood coloring the bottom of the shower. She stood in the shower, trying to hold him up.

"Baby?" she asked as he ran the water through his hair and beard. "What's going on? What happened?"

***

Chris looked at her, not wanting to reply, but knowing that he would ultimately have to. The mess had grown out of control, and everything that had once made sense to him now seemed like the dirty remains being sucked away in the drain below him. The shower had awakened him, but only enough for him to stand up on his own.

***

She held a towel out for him as he stepped out of the water.

"I need you to know something, Chris," she said as he looked up at her. "I love you, Chris."

Chris looked at her and started to interrupt her, but she continued.

"I don't know how, and I don't know why, Chris, but I have fallen in love with you." Then she added, "But..."

Chris sat on the end of the bed, pulled his hair back into a band, and listened to her.

"I love you, Chris, Preach, or whatever you call yourself," she said sarcastically, almost agitated. "But I will not let you hurt me. I didn't want a man in my life, Chris. But for whatever reason, God allowed you to come into it. I need you to know that I love you, but if you don't love me, I want you to go and not come back."

Tears slowly ran down her cheeks.

Chris looked at the carpet and then back up at her. She started to say something else, but he stopped her.

"Hannah, I fell in love with you the first time I saw you," he said as he stood. "I have loved you my whole life. It just took me forty years to find you."

He pulled up the clean jeans that she had set out on the bed.

"You are my home, Hannah," he said, looking at her.

Hannah leaned back on the wall, watching him.

"I love you enough to not allow my hell to ruin your heaven, Hannah," he said as he pulled his boots on.

"Where are you going? You're hurt," she said, stepping toward him.

He blocked her with an outstretched arm.

"Stop," he commanded.

She looked at him, anger and sadness in her eyes.

"Hannah, I'll come by tomorrow and get my things," he said as he tried to walk out the bedroom door.

Hannah grabbed his arm, stopping him.

He looked down at the soft hand that was grasping his tattooed arm and said, "I'm not good, baby. My life is a mess, and you are better than this."

He gently pulled away from her.

"If you love me, stay," she said, fighting off more tears.

Chris didn't look back at her. He made his way down the stairs and to the door.

Hannah stood in the doorway of the bedroom at the top of the stairs, watching him. Then she moved down the stairs, going after him.

***

Chris didn't look back as he stepped onto the front porch. The rain was still pouring outside. His cut was ruined; the black buffalo hide was torn and sliced. He emptied the contents of his pockets to retrieve his Zippo, and a single cigar remained in the blood-stained container.

"I'm sorry…" he said as he looked back at the closest thing to love he had had in a long time.

She was "home" to him, but right now he was confused on what the right thing to do was. Part of him wanted to stay, while the other part wanted him to leave. He lit his cigar and headed out into the street. The trees gave him cover from the elements as he made his way back to the SUV that he had stolen from the FARM.

***

"Preach!" she yelled from her driveway.

She was standing in the rain barefooted, the rain soaking through her thin clothes again. She ran down the street to where he stood.

"Preach, I love you. I love you whether you're a mess or not. I can't just let you go," she said as she grabbed him, and their eyes met.

"Hannah, go home. I can't give you what you want," he said as he took a draw from his cigar.

"Do you know what first Corinthians, chapter thirteen, verse eight says?" Hannah asked.

Chris looked poised as he said, "No, Hannah, I don't know what it says."

She pulled his face into her hands and said, "Baby, it says, 'Love never fails.'"

Chris pulled away from her and looked out into the distance.

"I'm not giving up on you, Chris. Home is right here waiting on you," she said, looking at him.

"Hannah… I can't."

He turned back to her and pulled her to him, kissing her strongly and then letting her go and walking off into the darkness.

Hannah stood and watched him walk away.

"Please, Father…" she prayed.

Deep inside of her spirit, she could hear a sweet, soft voice.

"Be still, and know that I am God…"

Hannah closed her eyes, and when she reopened them, Chris was gone.

"I will trust you, Father," she whispered. "It hurts, and I don't like it. But I will keep my eyes on you."

She turned and headed back to her house.

"Father, please watch over him," she prayed as she took one last look in the direction she had last seen Chris walking.

Chapter 47

Sacrifice

Chris pulled the SUV into the old church parking lot. It had only been a short while since he had met the pastor here. He was running away, but he was running in circles. There was no escape, only more distractions that hid the truth. Chris's fears. The ghost haunting his dreams. He had just learned that the most horrific nightmare was reality. Brothers, friends, and allies were the ones creating the chaos within him. The very core of his beliefs had been tainted by corruption. Everything was a lie. His very existence was fantasy. Yet he remained.

His mind rallied, trying to regroup from all the drugs running through his veins.

"Hannah, I love you," he cried as he stared up at the old church building.

"Lord, if you are really there, let me come back and know the truth," he cried.

Silence echoed around him. He opened the door of the SUV and staggered toward the large wooden doors of the church like a homeless drunk. He was surprised when the doors opened. He looked at his watch. 12:05 a.m.

If you only have five minutes at midnight, you can accomplish anything, his mother said, speaking through his spirit.

He grabbed the edge of the first pew, trying to stay standing as he walked to the altar.

Do This in Remembrance of Me were the words carved into the wooden table stationed in front of the podium. Behind that were several rows of pews for the church choir. Chris's eyes looked above and beyond the wood and the crimson colors of the old church's interior. High above, surrounded by stained-glass Christian artwork, was a large wooden cross. He strained to focus on it.

Where is Jesus?

Chris heard the footsteps behind him and reached for his weapons. His body was too weak to fight, but he forced himself to accept the challenge. His eyes fought the shadows in his blurred vision. He fought to focus on the bodies moving toward where he knelt on the floor.

"Christopher, it's okay," a voice said, comforting his thoughts.

"Marcus?" he questioned. The thoughts of betrayal raced through his mind. "Not you, too."

"Christopher..." Marcus said again.

Chris fought to stay alert.

"Do you know why you came back to Valley Town?" the voice of Apostle James Wallaby asked.

Chris's intoxicated delusions were forcing him to the brink of insanity.

"What is wrong with me?" he screamed.

Marcus and Pastor James stayed a safe distance away, but they formed a protective barrier for their loved one.

"That note, the one written in red..." Pastor James said.

Chris fought harder to remain conscious.

"Mama..." Chris wept.

"That's right, kid. Your mama wrote that note. But we have no idea how you got it in Murphy," Marcus said.

"Before your mother passed, she started a movement. Her vision was to love those that the world had seemingly forgotten," Pastor James said.

Chris searched the shadows of the church to find the man's face.

"God wants you to return to your calling, son," Pastor James continued.

Chris's mind was twisting out of control. The ghost that haunted him shot in and out of his mind's eye. He began slicing with his arms, hitting only air.

"Christopher, you can't live by the sword. Scripture warns us that if we live by the sword, we will die by the sword. We have to choose what sword we live by: God's Word or cold steel that is lifeless. Son, there is an old man inside of you that you may not even realize is there, but he is. He died a long time ago, Christopher. Only you can allow him to live now. He is waiting on you. He lives off the remains of your failures, fears, and worries. He feeds on the past, the things that you have left behind. The darkness is his domain, Christopher."

Chris dropped to his knees, the blade falling to the floor.

"I don't understand," he said, pleading with those surrounding him.

His eyes focused, but he only saw images of figures surrounding him. He surrendered. He was outnumbered, too weak to continue.

"What is rule number nineteen, Christopher?" Marcus asked.

Chris felt strength trying to surface.

"Neva tap…" he slurred.

"The enemy you're fighting waits on the darkness to fall around you. He waits on your fears to rise up in your thoughts. He will call on you, Christopher. He will not give up until he beats you down," Pastor James said.

"Who are you to me?" Chris asked, trying to find answers.

"The old man is the enemy within you. He knows that you have the answers, but the answers are in you. The truth lies in the darkness of what you feel is lost. You have to let go of the idea that you are unforgivable. The sword you have could slay him, and he is aware of it. But you are the only one who can use it."

Chris looked out at what seemed to be hundreds of figures surrounding him. The two men in front of him, Marcus to his left and Pastor James to his right, seemed to be the only ones communicating.

"Don't step out into a battle you can't win solo. He knows what strengthens you, and he knows the weaknesses you try to hide," Marcus said. "You have been gifted with talents. You are a leader. You are a warrior. You fear nothing the world has thrown at you. The enemy knows that he can't ever have your soul. But if you allow the darkness to overcome you, he will come in and rip the foundations out from under you. He will gladly rob you of the freedom you hold inside of you."

Chris's eyes seemed to open. Not his physical eyes, but his spiritual eyes. The room hosted what seemed to be a legion of angelic beings, but in the windows, and just beyond the large wooden doors, his mind's eye saw images of evil creatures clawing, biting, and slobbering to reach him.

"Son, you have been called. You are a prophet unto the nations," Marcus said, pleading with him.

"The note wasn't calling you back to Valley Town alone. It was calling you back to your purpose," Pastor James said.

"Your nickname is 'Preacher,' so step back into that calling!" Marcus exclaimed. "It's your time. Preach to those lost sons and daughters. Reach out to those searching for the truth, those that society has rejected. The convicts, the addicts, and those lost in the webs of delusion."

Chris's eyes filled with tears, and he cried, "But God can't use me. I'm lost."

Marcus put his hand on Chris's shoulder and said, "My son, your first words were spot on. 'But God…' But God used a stuttering, self-conscious murderer to lead the children of Israel out of Egyptian slavery. But God used a lying cheat to create a nation. But God used a stubborn, hot-headed fisherman to spread the Gospel to thousands in one day alone. But God used a shepherd boy to be king and a man after His own heart. But the best 'But God' is when He used a poor carpenter to marry a virgin who gave birth to a Savior of the world. But God!"

Chris bowed his head and confessed, "I've done too much to deserve forgiveness."

Pastor James let out a peaceful laugh and said, "God's grace is not deserved. He gives it as freely as He gives His forgiveness for sins. God's mercy is for what we do deserve, and His forgiveness overcomes."

Chris sat, almost defeated.

"God has called you. He has placed a vision and a purpose within you. What is it?" the pastor asked.

Chris looked up again at the room around him. Now nothing remained except the two men kneeling on both sides of him.

"The Lost Highway, searching for the Lost Boys," Chris whispered.

"Then let's get to it!" the pastor said with excitement.

Chris and the two men bowed their heads, and Chris opened up his heart to prayer. He was reminded of the story of the prodigal son returning home.

Home…

Chapter 48

No Goodbyes

The cold November rain fell steadily as the large crowd stood next to the waters of Lake Weiss. Some of the men held umbrellas for the women, but most stood silently as they waited for the pallbearers to remove the caskets from the wagon.

Chris stood back and watched, feeling reluctant. The last time he had stood in this field was the day he lay his mother to rest. The emotions rocked through him now. Oddly, though, he wasn't thinking of his mother. The love in him was growing like a virus. Like an uncontrollable fire.

Hannah, I wish you were here beside me. I need you.

He looked down at the ring he had placed on his finger as a symbol of his faith and the love that would forever guide him and perhaps even haunt him.

Everyone looked like they felt peace rather than agony or loss. They each had their own stories of why they stood here right now. They all had a few things in common, though: Brotherhood, Sisterhood, and Family.

Chris looked at the screen of his phone. The notes he had prepared lit up the screen. A text came in, and he opened it up to read it.

I love you, and I'm right here waiting, the text from Hannah read, shocking him.

How did she know?

The funeral director motioned to Chris. The Defensores de la Fe choir began to sing softly as Bishop Cruz and Chris made their way to the front of the congregation. The bishop whispered something in Chris's ear and turned to sit. Chris stepped up to the podium. He grabbed his old Bible and looked out at the diverse mix of people amassed before him.

Two caskets were positioned in front of him. To his right was a group of Lost Boys. To the left was a group of other families. He cleared his thoughts, took a deep breath, and addressed the crowd.

"Family, Brothers, Sisters, and friends. Today, we lay to rest two men who deserve our respect and our loyalty, even in the wake of their deaths. These two Brothers gave their all to protect what they believed was sacred and worthy. These men of valor did not turn away from the fight, but boldly raced forward to bring others home safely, ending an era of torment for many souls. Though they may be gone, they will never be forgotten."

He looked into the faces attending the ceremony.

"Let us pray," he continued.

The crowd bowed their heads together, and Chris took another deep breath.

"Most gracious Heavenly Father, into Your hands we commend our fallen in the sure and certain hope that, together with all who have died in Christ, they shall rise again with Him. We give You thanks for the blessings You bestowed upon them in this life. They are signs to us of Your goodness and of our fellowship with the saints in Christ Jesus, the Messiah.

"Merciful Lord, turn toward us and hear our prayers. Open the gates of heaven to your servants and help those who remain to comfort one another with assurances of faith. Let us be faithful until we all meet again in Christ and are with You and those who have gone before us into eternity.

"In peace, let us take our fallen to their place of rest. May the angels lead our fallen into Paradise. May the martyrs come to welcome you and take you to the Holy City, the New Jerusalem. May those of us left behind forever ride in Your light, Lord. May we have your forgiveness. May we bring You glory in all that we do. With prayerful thanks, we raise our right hand of fellowship and call to arms all that will hear us. In Christ Jesus…"

The crowd responded together, one voice representing a massive crowd of witnesses, "Ani ma amin."

Chris opened his eyes and scanned the crowd again.

"There are no goodbyes, only 'I'll see ya when we get there.' Today, we amass together as Family! We stand together as one. I am my Brother's keeper and my Sister's protector."

Chris placed his right fist on his chest, looking out into the Brother's faces. They all followed his lead.

"Who are we?" he yelled.

The Brothers roared together, "We are Kingdom Sons! Men of Valor! Brothers forever! Aroo! Aroo! Aroo!"

Chris looked down at his Bible. It was open on 1 Corinthians 13. Placed in the crease was a small sticky note attached to a photo. I love you. Come back to me, it read. He looked at the picture and smiled.

"My love, my Queen…" he whispered as he smiled to himself.

He looked into the crowd. In the front row sat Mac, Dolly, and Anna. Ruth stood behind a wheelchair at the end of the front row. Marcus sat with his arms crossed, grasping his old King James, smiling at Chris.

"Welcome home," Marcus whispered.

The cold November morning found more than the heaven's rain falling. The reign of a new Brotherhood was born.

The Brothers walked to their motorcycles. Their leathers now hosted new colors. The top patch read Kingdom Sons. The center patch showed a raven perched on a cross, carrying a rose in. The bottom patch read Forgiven.

Chris knew that the nightmare was far from over. Somewhere out there, Señor Cruz watched his movements. It wouldn't be long before they resurfaced. Chris would be ready.

Two federal agents waited on his right. Chris acknowledged them with a slight grin. His father and brother stood next to the agents, and he winked at his family.

"Let's do this," he said, walking beside the agents.

Chris's life was never going to be the same, but at least for now there was unity. As he began to sit down in the car, he noticed a figure standing in the distance. He smiled.

Home.

She saw beyond my mess,
and loved me regardless.
Cap and Tina October 2015

Acknowledgements

As I have worked on this project, I have found throughout the process that many of my favorite people, friends, Brothers, Sisters, and mentors have been portrayed as characters. I give my heartfelt and sincere gratitude to so many people who have walked with me through reality and through the fiction that made up this body of work.

I give so much to praise my Heavenly Father, the healer of my mind, body, and soul. I'm thankful for the cleansing power of His grace, which I didn't deserve, and His mercy, which prevented the things that I did deserve to have happen to me. It's through Him and Him alone that I find freedom. True freedom.

It is said, "The imagination is the greatest gift of God." I believe this to be true, because throughout Scripture, it was the hope and faith that fueled the imaginations of God's people, and they were able to ask Him for the impossible. What is impossible for man is possible for our sovereign Heavenly Father. He has blessed me with so many things, and an imagination is one of them. I am blessed to turn what was not into something that is.

If you would humor me for just a few moments, I would like to talk to you about a truth that is missing from our society. We are losing a battle that could be won by utilizing the right tools.

Statute number fifteen in the Lost Highway / Kingdom Sons Fearless Daughters Ministries says, "Knowledge is power."

But I want to amend that statute to this: "Utilized knowledge is wisdom. All knowledge a man has is pointless if it's not put into action."

Scripture says, "…faith without works is dead…" I emphasize this statement. Knowledge without utilization is a waste and lacks the power to overcome anything at all.

So, what is utilized knowledge? It's learning to do less trying and more dying. It's understanding the truths of wisdom and overcoming the lies that have blinded us as a society. It's understanding that "I can't" but "He can."

I'm not trying to get on a soapbox and proclaim that the world is failing to see the truth, though many people are. I'm here to ask you to look past the pretty images that we call church and try, for a moment, to see what Jesus came to accomplish, He came to heal and restore mankind to Himself. The Jesus of the Bible came to die on a Roman Cross for all of mankind, not just for the picture of the "American Dream."

He came to reach the lost ones: the outcasts, the addicts, the sluts, the liars, and the thieves. He loved the poor, gave truth to the liars, and gave honor to the thieves. He reached down to lift up the sluts and those living in sin, saying, "...go, and sin no more." He laid hands on the unclean and gave them life. He came to show us how to live as He did: with love.

I want to be like that. I want to see past the fake religious practices and bring life to those searching for something real. Ephesians teaches us to imitate Christ, but so often we look so much more like the world than believers.

He came to bleed and die, and yet we found Him living and spending His time with those considered unworthy and condemned by society. The Jesus we read about in John's Gospel came for everyone. He came to heal those in need of healing, to feed those who were hungry, and to give water to those who thirsted. He was not just there for those who were able to put more money into the offering plates and bring popularity to the churches.

As God began opening up my eyes to the vision that began forming the foundations of The Lost Highways Ministries and Kingdom Sons Outreach ministry, I realized I wanted to be more like the Jesus of the Bible and less like the religious moguls of modern practices of success and popularity. I began dying more to my own ideas and understanding, and in my blindness I realized that all of the "trying' was in vain. All of my "knowledge" and "understanding" of God's Holy Word was rubbish as long as I failed to understand and utilize the truth of His unfailing grace and mercy in my life.

The Jesus that I serve seeks out the outcasts more than the arrogant churchgoers who turn up their noses to the lost souls seeking His love. There is a Lost Highway out there that leads us into the darkest avenues, dirtiest streets, and, in some cases, mud pits and wildernesses, yet these places are full of God's children, and they are waiting for, hoping for, and seeking something real to call "Home."

We have to remember that Jesus was once considered a criminal. He died as a common outcast on a Roman Cross. But that's only part of the Gospel. I think that we miss such a big part of the truth of the Cross. We follow Him to the Cross where He died, but we forget that He rose up on the third day and is alive today!

If we are to truly follow Him, it's important that we turn away from our old ways, rise up and live, and seek out those seeking His truth. He rose up so that we, too, could rise up out of the murky clay and stand upon the rock of His love. We are called to be His hands, His eyes, and His lips. We are called to be His voice and His healing touch as we seek out those seeking.

The questions remain:

Will we cross the street to avoid the beggars and the sick?

Will we turn our eyes away from those held captive in sexual slavery?

Will we be politically correct and look the other way when our own kids are being taught that sex outside of marriage, abortion, and homosexuality are things to celebrate?

Or will we be more like Jesus and bring love into the lost avenues, streets, and alleyways, sharing with those who seek true love and compassion?

The truth: Jesus came to pick a fight.

He did, and He won.

It's my hope that we can reach out to society's outcasts and show them true love, God's unconditional love. I hope that we can teach the addicts how to overcome instead of relapsing again and again. I hope we can show those lost in sexual perversion that there is hope. I hope we can mentor our youth correctly, showing them real love and giving them a better way than a life of crime or a life behind the wire.

Society would rather lock away the outcasts and keep them out of sight, but that creates a much more dangerous situation. By shutting our eyes, as a society, to the messes around us, we allow greater messes to build, opening up more room for more messes to follow.

Where are the fathers? Where are the teachers? Where are the prayer warriors battling on their knees?

That is what this project is all about. It's not about the dramatic messes that we create with false hope and faulty freedom. This is about realizing that even in the biggest messes, God is there, ready to bring light to our darkness. Because in the end, only God can bless a mess.

And it's in the "But God" moments of life that we find truth. It's not in our trying but in our dying to selfish ambitions that will change the 'But God?' from a question and into an explanation: "But God took a mess I made and brought forth His very best in me!"

Our towns, our cities, and our valleys are filled with searching, lost, and seemingly hopeless outcasts. Isn't it time to open our hearts to the least of us? Just as our Savior did for you and me? We must remember that we, too, were once outcasts, lost and condemned to death yet seeking the same truth, the same resurrection power that the Cross gives those who put their hope and trust in Jesus.

It is my sincere hope and prayer that together we will impact the world by following the commandment that was left for all believers to follow: Go and bring the lost home.

May God bless each of you as you travel down the Lost Highways of this life, and may you reach out to bring others home with you.

One God, One King

In Christ's Love, For His Kingdom!!

- The Preacher

Proof that God can bless a mess.
Cap and Tina 2020

Bible quotations in the book

(a) Psalm 23:1 KJV
(b) Psalm 23:4 KJV
(c) 2 Kings 6:16 KJV
(d) Psalm 23:1 KJV
(e) (f) (g) Jeremiah 1:5 KJV
(h) Jeremiah 1:8 KJV
(i) 1 Corinthians 13:4-8 NIV
(j) Zechariah 10:1 NIV
(k) Zechariah 10:6 NIV
(l) (m) 1 Corinthians 13:8 NIV
(n) Psalm 46:10 NIV
(o) James 2:20 KJV
(p) John 8:11 KJV

Other References:

"Unclouded Day"
Gospel Hymnal written by Josiah Kelly Alwood in 1879.

"Amazing Grace"
Christian Hymn words written by John Newton in 1772.

"Do not go gentle into that good night"
Poem written by Sir Dylan Thomas in 1947.

My best friend, battle buddy, my Peanut

For more information about Kingdom Sons Outreach,
Talking Rock Outpost and Bushcraft school
or merchandise contact
Kingdomsons1119@gmail.com

CPSIA information can be obtained
at www.ICGtesting.com
Printed in the USA
FSHW021814260221
78945FS